MYSTERIOUS ✦ DEATHS

The Little Princes in the Tower

by William W. Lace

Lucent Books
P.O. Box 289011, San Diego, CA 92198-9011

These titles are included in the *Mysterious Deaths* series:

Butch Cassidy
Amelia Earhart
John F. Kennedy
Abraham Lincoln

The Little Princes in the Tower
Malcolm X
Marilyn Monroe
Mozart

Cover Design: Carl Franzen

Library of Congress Cataloging-in-Publication Data

Lace, William, W.
      The little princes in the Tower / by William W. Lace
            p. cm.—(Mysterious Deaths)
      Includes bibliographical references and index.
      Summary: Discusses the deaths of twelve-year-old Crown Prince
Edward V of England and his younger brother who mysteriously disappeared during the Hundred Years War.
      ISBN 1-56006-262-2 (alk. paper)
      1. Edward V, King of England, 1470–1483—Juvenile literature. 2. Great
Britain—History—Richard III, 1483–1485—Juvenile literature. 3. Death—England—London—History—16th century—Juvenile literature. 4. Great
Britain—Kings and rulers—Biography—Juvenile literature. 5. Richard Duke
of York, 1473-1483—Juvenile literature. 6. Princes—Great Britain—Biography—Juvenile literature. 7. Tower of London (London, England)—Juvenile
literature. [1. Edward V, King of England, 1470–1483. 2. Richard, Duke of York,
1473–1483. 3. Great Britain—History—Richard III, 1483—1485. 4. Kings,
queens, rulers, etc.]
I. Title.   II. Series.
DA259.L33   1997
942.04'5—dc20   96-21509
                                                                                    CIP
                                                                                    AC

Printed in the U.S.A.
Copyright © 1997 by Lucent Books, Inc.
P.O. Box 289011, San Diego, CA 92198-9011

Contents

Haunting Human History

The *Mysterious Deaths* series focuses on nine individuals whose deaths have never been fully explained. Some are figures from the distant past; others are far more contemporary. Yet all of them remain fascinating as much for who they were and how they lived as for how they died. Their lives were characterized by fame and fortune, tragedy and triumph, secrets that led to acute vulnerability. Our enduring fascination with these stories, then, is due in part to the lives of the victims and in part to the array of conflicting facts and opinions, as well as the suspense, that surrounds their deaths.

Some of the people profiled in the *Mysterious Deaths* series were controversial political figures who lived and died in the public eye. John F. Kennedy, Abraham Lincoln, and Malcolm X were all killed in front of crowds as guards paid to protect them were unable to stop their murders. Despite all precautions, their assassins found ample opportunity to carry out their crimes. In each case, the assassins were tried and convicted. So what remains mysterious? As the reader will discover, everything.

The two women in the series, Marilyn Monroe and Amelia Earhart, are equally well remembered. Both died at the heights of their careers; both, from all appearances, had everything to live for. Yet their deaths have also been shrouded in mystery. While there are simple explanations—Monroe committed suicide, Earhart's plane crashed—the public has never been able to accept them. The more researchers dig into the deaths, the more mysterious evidence they unearth. Monroe's predilection for affairs with prominent politicians may have led to her death. Earhart, brash and cavalier, may have been involved in a government plot that collapsed around her. And these theories do not exhaust the mysterious possibilities that continue to puzzle researchers.

The circumstances of the deaths of the remaining figures in the *Mysterious Deaths* series—Richard III's nephews Edward and

Richard; the brilliant composer Wolfgang Mozart; and the infamous bank robber Butch Cassidy—are less well known but no less fascinating.

For example, what are almost surely the skeletons of the little princes Edward and Richard were found buried at the foot of a stairway in the Tower of London in 1674. To many, the discovery proved beyond a doubt that their evil uncle, Richard III, murdered them to attain the throne. Yet others find Richard wrongly accused, the obvious scapegoat. The mysterious tale of their deaths—full of dungeons, plots, and treachery—is still intriguing today.

In the history books, Wolfgang Mozart died in poverty from a consumptive-like disease. Yet there are reports and rumors, snatches of information culled from distant records, that Mozart may have died from a slow poisoning. Who could have wanted to murder the famous composer? And why?

Finally, bank robber Butch Cassidy's death couldn't have been less mysterious—shot to death by military police in Bolivia along with his companion, the Sundance Kid. Then why did members of Butch Cassidy's family and numerous others swear to have seen him, in full health, in the United States years after his supposed death?

These true-life whodunits are filled with tantalizing "what ifs?" What if Kennedy had used the bulletproof plastic hood that his Secret Servicemen had ready? What if Lincoln had decided not to attend the theater—which he did only to please his wife? What if Monroe's friend, Peter Lawford, receiving no answer to his persistent calls, had gone to her house, as he wanted to do? These questions frustrate us as well as testify to a haunting aspect of human history—the way that seemingly insignificant decisions can alter its course.

A Struggle for the Throne

King Edward V had the shortest and most unhappy reign of any ruler in the long history of England. He was just twelve years old when his father, Edward IV, died on April 9, 1483. Only seventy-seven days later, his uncle Richard, duke of Gloucester, seized the throne.

Although numbered among England's kings, Edward V never actually ruled. He was never crowned. For most of his short reign, he was a virtual prisoner of his uncle in the Tower of London. Even after he was joined there by his younger brother Richard, duke of York, he was said by the few people allowed to see him to be sad and melancholy, as though preparing for death.

Edward V holds the dubious honor of having the shortest, most unhappy reign in history, as well as having the cruel fate to stand in the way of his uncle, King Richard III.

Edward IV (left) angered some of his strongest supporters when he married Elizabeth Woodville (right), pictured here with their two sons.

Edward had good reason to worry. Shortly before the coronation of their uncle as King Richard III, he and his brother disappeared from public view. The two boys were never seen again. When and how they met their deaths—at whose hands and on whose orders—was one of the great mysteries of their time, and so it remains.

While the circumstances of Edward V's death were mysterious, those of his birth were turbulent. His father, even though he was king, had been forced to flee the country. His mother had taken refuge in a church.

The year was 1470, and the houses of Lancaster and York, branches of the Plantagenet family, which had ruled England since 1154, had been fighting for possession of the throne for fifteen years. The struggle was called the Wars of the Roses because of the symbols supposedly used by the two families—the white rose of York and the red rose of Lancaster.

Edward IV of the house of York had declared himself king in 1461 and defeated the Lancastrians at the Battle of Towton. Three years later, however, Edward angered his strongest supporter, the earl of Warwick, by secretly marrying Elizabeth Woodville, a woman from a large but obscure family. Edward gave members of the new queen's family important positions, making them rivals of Warwick.

7

In this well-known painting of the princes Edward and Richard, the two clasp their hands, fearfully awaiting their fate in the Tower of London.

Birth of the Princes

In 1470 Warwick formed an alliance with the Lancastrians and invaded England from France. Edward had to flee from the country to avoid being taken prisoner. Elizabeth, who was pregnant, took refuge with her three daughters in the great London church Westminster Abbey. It was there on November 2 that Prince Edward was born.

In 1471 Edward IV won back his crown, defeating the Lancastrians at Barnet and Tewksbury. He was a strong, wise ruler, and the years between 1471 and 1483 were mostly peaceful. He and Elizabeth had a second son, Richard, on August 17, 1473, and two more daughters.

The house of Lancaster was all but extinguished. Its last, faint hope was a Welshman named Henry Tudor, who was living in exile in France. It seemed that for the house of York to be destroyed, it would have to destroy itself, which is exactly what happened.

England might have continued in peace had Edward IV lived a normal life span. He died at forty, however, his body worn out by years of rich food and wine, and young Edward was next in line. As usually happened when a king died before his oldest son had reached adulthood, a struggle broke out over who would control the boy. On one side was his uncle; on the other were his mother and her relatives, the Woodvilles. The innocent victims of the struggle were the princes—Edward and Richard—who entered the Tower of London in 1483 and never came out, at least not alive.

The Skeletons in the Staircase

Grim and gray, the Tower of London has stood on the banks of the River Thames for more than nine hundred years. It was first a crude wooden fort built in 1066 to give William of Normandy—William the Conqueror—a safe place to stay in a defeated city while waiting to be crowned.

Twelve years later, the wooden fort was replaced with a huge stone castle, ninety feet high with walls fifteen feet thick. This castle, called the White Tower after King Henry III had it whitewashed in the 1200s, eventually became surrounded with a series of towers and walls, all of which came to be known as the Tower of London.

The Tower has served many purposes. It has been a palace where kings lived and a fort in which they took refuge in times of danger. It has been a depository for state papers and for the royal treasury. It was used as an observatory by astronomers and, as late as 1834, as a zoo.

The Tower of London is best known, however, as a prison where both the most distinguished and most dangerous prisoners have been kept. Many a man—and some women, as well—have gone from cells in the Tower to the hangman's rope or the headsman's block. Others—those whose deaths it was thought best to keep from public view—went into the Tower and simply disappeared.

King Edward V and his younger brother were by no means the first to vanish within the Tower's walls. King Henry VI, deposed by Edward IV, was murdered there in 1471, no one knows how. In 1478, Edward IV's brother George, duke of Clarence, was executed for treason. The story—never proved—is that he was drowned in a barrel of Malmsey, his favorite wine.

When the young princes disappeared in 1483, rumors quickly spread that they had been killed. Their uncle, Richard III, was suspected, but nothing could be proved, however, and two years later,

Richard was killed at the Battle of Bosworth. Henry Tudor succeeded him, as King Henry VII, and tried to solve the mystery. Henry's efforts were motivated by a personal desire to close the books on the case: he feared that the princes, if still alive, might challenge his right to the crown. More than fifteen years later, someone confessed to the crime, but no trace of the princes could be found.

False Alarms

Gradually, the mystery was forgotten. Then, in the early 1600s, a small skeleton was found in a pipe that ran underneath the Tower. People first thought it was one of the princes, but an examination showed that the bones were the remains of an ape that had somehow escaped from the royal zoo.

In 1647 two small skeletons were found in the Tower itself, in a small room that had been walled up. Since, according to one of the stories circulating at the time of the princes' disappearance, the boys had been sealed up in a chamber and allowed to starve to death, those who found the two skeletons thought they had found

The Tower of London is most famous for the days when it was used as a prison. It was here that the princes mysteriously disappeared.

The Tower of London

The Tower of London, which figures so prominently in the story of the princes, had its start when a king of England didn't feel that it was safe for him to enter his own capital city. Even though William I, known as William the Conqueror, had been invited by the leading men of the kingdom to rule over them after his victory in the Battle of Hastings in 1066, he would not enter London until a fort had been built in which he would be secure.

The site chosen was on the Thames River just inside the city wall on its east side. The first castle was of the type known as "motte and bailey," a mound with a wooden tower on top surrounded by a high stockade fence. Only when construction was finished would William enter London.

The Tower was one of several large, stone castles built by William I and his Normans after they conquered England. The Normans were few in number and were in a hostile land. For security, they used a technique they had perfected in Normandy, a part of France, building huge castles from which they could control the surrounding countryside.

Within a year, William ordered a Norman monk, Gundulf of Bec, to begin rebuilding the wooden fort in stone. Construction took more than ten years, but the result was a huge, square castle with a tower on each corner.

Soon, the fort became known as the Tower of London; it remains one of the most famous buildings in the world. The part built by Gundulf was whitewashed and is called the White Tower. The term "Tower of London" as used today refers not only to the White Tower, but to the entire complex of other towers and walls built around this early structure over the centuries.

the princes. They were wrong. Doctors examined the bones and said they were those of children about six and eight years old—far too young to be the sons of Edward IV.

Then, in 1674, King Charles II ordered the area around the White Tower cleared "of all contiguous buildings." By this he meant a collection of buildings that had been constructed against the south side of the White Tower, including the old royal apartments. Among this group of buildings was a small tower—about twenty feet square—containing a staircase. For centuries, English kings and their families had used this private staircase to reach a doorway into the second story of the White Tower. Through this doorway was the Chapel of St. John the Evangelist, a favorite place for worship.

The workmen demolished the tower and pulled down the staircase. When they began digging up the staircase's foundations, they discovered a wooden chest buried about ten feet below the ground. In the chest were two small skeletons, one slightly larger than the other. The larger skeleton was on its back; the smaller one was face down on top of the larger.

Once more, it was believed the princes had been found. An eyewitness wrote:

> This day I, standing by the opening, saw working men dig out of a stairway in the White Tower the bones of those two Princes who were foully murdered by Richard III. They were small bones of lads in their teens, and there were pieces of rag and velvet about them. . . . [They were] fully recognized to be the bones of those two princes.

And one of the laborers, John Gibbon, wrote, "July 17 anno 1674 in diggin some foundacons in ye Tower, were discovered ye bodies of Edw 5 and his brother murdered 1483. I my selfe handled y Bones Especially ye Kings Skull. Ye other wch was lesser broken in ye digging."

"At the Stair Foot"

This time, there seemed to be little doubt that the remains of Edward V and Richard, duke of York, had been found. One reason was that the skeletons had been found under a staircase. According to the most detailed and widely believed account of the princes' deaths, Sir Thomas More's *History of King Richard III*, written in the early 1500s, the bodies were buried "at the stair foot, meetly [moderately] deep in the ground." Charles II ordered the bones to be examined by the royal surgeon and other scientists. All agreed they were the skeletons of the princes.

The skeletons remained in the Tower for four years. Sightseers came to gaze on them. A few of the bones were sent to a museum at Oxford University. Finally, Charles II decided that the skeletons should go to Westminster Abbey, the large church near London where many English kings were buried. He ordered his chief architect, Christopher Wren, to "provide a white marble coffin for the supposed bodies of the Princes."

Wren designed an altar of black and white marble. An urn, or large jar, containing the skeletons was buried underneath the altar. The inscription, which still may be read by visitors to the abbey, read:

> Here lie interred the remains of Edward V, King of England, and Richard, Duke of York, whose long desired and much sought after bones, after above [more than] a hundred and ninety years, were found by most certain tokens, deep

A painting depicts the murder of the little princes Edward V and his younger brother, Richard, at the hands of Richard III. The painting shows the brothers being dragged down to the bottom of a staircase—it is under these same stairs that two small skeletons were found in 1674.

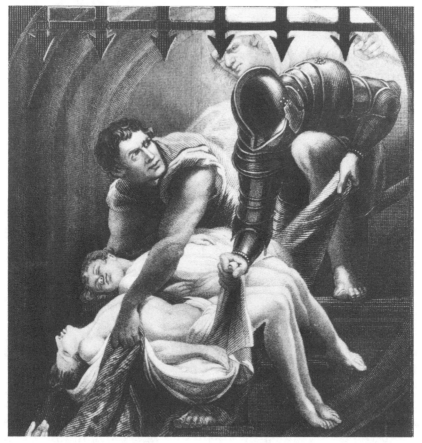

The final resting place of the skeletons thought to be those of the little princes. The graves and the monument are in the Henry VII Chapel at Westminster Abbey.

interred [buried] under the rubbish of the stairs that led up to the Chapel of the White Tower, on the 17th of July in the year of our Lord 1674. Charles the Second, a most merciful prince, having compassion upon their hard fortune, performed the funeral rites of these unhappy Princes among the tombs of their ancestors, anno Domini [in the year of our Lord] 1678.

No description of the "most certain tokens" is available.

Remaining Doubts

And yet, doubts as to the identity of the skeletons persisted. Some historians through the centuries have claimed that the princes had not been murdered, but escaped. The bones, they said, were not those of the princes at all. In 1728 a scientist, Thomas Hearne, went to Oxford University to see the bones that had been sent there. They could not be found, although a longtime museum employee remembered seeing them and said they had been "very small, particularly the finger bones."

The argument raged back and forth. Finally, in the early 1900s, people on both sides of the question requested that the bones be removed from the tomb and studied. New techniques of science and medicine, they said, would settle the case. Since Westminster Abbey was under royal control, the king's permission was needed. In 1933 King George V gave his authorization.

Westminster Abbey

Westminster Abbey, where King Edward V was born and where his mother, brother, and sisters sought refuge from Richard III, had been built more than four hundred years earlier by another King Edward, the Saxon monarch Edward the Confessor. Edward was intensely religious and made the building of the abbey his lifework.

The site was the Isle of Thorney west of London, a bramble-covered piece of ground surrounded by the Thames and Tyburn Rivers. Traditionally, the first church on the island had been founded by Saberht, first Christian king of the East Saxons. It was dedicated to St. Peter, and the saint himself was supposed to have appeared to consecrate it.

Edward, who admired the culture of Normandy, had the church designed on the Norman pattern, in the shape of a cross, with a main tower and two lesser towers. As it grew, it came to be known by the people as West Minster, as opposed to the East Minster, St. Paul's Cathedral in London.

Edward was too ill to attend the dedication, on December 28, 1065, and in fact died a week later. His successor, Harold, became the first English king to be crowned at Westminster. William the Conqueror was also crowned there, as has been every monarch since. Two kings, however, were never crowned—Edward VIII, who gave up the throne in 1936 to marry a divorced woman, and Edward V, who was murdered before his coronation had a chance to take place.

Edward the Confessor was the first of many English kings to be buried in Westminster Abbey. A shrine to him remains there, but the original building has all but disappeared. It was rebuilt mostly by William's great-great-great-grandson, Henry III, two hundred years later.

The bones were examined by Dr. Lawrence Tanner, a physician and Keeper of the Monuments at Westminster Abbey; by Professor William Wright, a surgeon and president of the Anatomical Society of Great Britain; and by Dr. George Northcroft, president of the British Dental Association. They first discovered that many animal bones were mixed among those of humans. Probably, souvenir hunters had taken some of the human bones during the four years between 1674 and 1678, substituting animal bones.

Enough human bones were left, however, for the scientists to say that the skeletons were those of two children, one four feet, ten inches tall and the other four feet, six and one-half inches tall. The experts could not say whether the bones were those of boys or girls, but said the similar structure of the bones of the faces indicated that the children could well have been related.

The scientists determined the ages at the time of death by studying both the bones and teeth. As children grow to adulthood, the cartilage in their bones gradually changes to bone tissue in a process known as ossification. Wright examined the degree of ossification in the skeletons. He placed their ages at the time of death from twelve to thirteen years for the older child and nine to eleven for the younger. In September 1483, Edward V would have been almost thirteen and Richard ten.

Signs of Disease

Northcroft agreed with Wright's conclusion, based on his own study of the extent to which permanent teeth had come in. Northcroft also discovered that the lower jaw of the older child showed evidence of a bone disease that would have been very painful. This might have made the boy appear sad and melancholy to those who saw him. Wright also found red stain on the facial bones of the older child. He said this was probably a bloodstain caused by suffocation.

Wright published his findings in 1934. He said that the evidence that the bones were those of the princes was "more conclusive than could, considering everything, reasonably have been expected." He added that "the evidence that the bones in the urn are those of the Princes is as conclusive as could be desired."

The findings were not as conclusive as everyone desired, namely the "revisionists," as historians who doubt that Richard III murdered his nephews are sometimes called. The key question for the revisionists was the ages of the princes when they died. If the early findings were correct and the bodies were, indeed, those of the princes, they must have been killed early in 1484 at the latest. If the findings were off, even by only a few years, the princes could have been alive when Richard III died on August 22, 1485. Obviously, then, it would be necessary to identify another suspect—perhaps Henry VII, who might have had the youths killed to eliminate them as possible rivals for the throne.

In later years, the revisionists have sought to have the urn reopened and the bones examined again. New scientific techniques, they claim, would make it possible to tell more about the skeletons. The findings published in 1934, however, satisfied the authorities at Westminster Abbey, who have refused all later requests to remove the skeletons.

Since he could not have access to the bones themselves, one of Richard III's biographers, Paul Murray Kendall, did the next best thing. In 1955 he submitted to a new team of experts the photographs that had been taken of the skeletons by Wright's team and the reports of the scientists.

Professor William Wright, surgeon and president of the Anatomical Society of Great Britain, was part of the team who investigated the alleged skeletons of the little princes. Wright concluded that the bodies were those of the princes.

In this dramatic painting, princes Edward V and Richard are led up the stairway of the Tower of London as Richard III looks on.

Dates in Doubt

Some members of the new team raised doubts about the 1934 findings, but none could prove that Tanner, Wright, and Northcroft had been wrong. One of Kendall's experts, Dr. Richard Lyne-Pirkis, later gave a lecture in which he went into great detail showing how the earlier investigators *might* have been wrong. He claimed that ages at the time of death cannot be pinpointed as accurately as was done in Professor Wright's report. Modern studies had shown, he said, that ossification takes place at widely varying rates in children, much depending on diet. According to Lyne-Pirkis, the ages might have been anywhere from seven to sixteen. Yet he could not say that the earlier investigations had been wrong and said, finally:

I'm afraid the conclusion . . . is not that we can be more accurate than Professor Wright. We are quite certain that we cannot be anything near as accurate as he thought he was. We cannot date the bones nearer than plus or minus two years in a good society, and if we have a mixed society, with some people getting good diets and some people getting poor diets, then it's more likely to be plus or minus three years. So that it would still be possible under those considerations for the Princes to have been alive when Richard III died on Bosworth Field.

Other authors have called on yet more experts for opinions. Most have agreed that the accuracy of the ages in the 1934 report was doubtful if only the ossification of the bones was considered. They have been more certain, based on the teeth, that the older child could not have been more than thirteen, but admit room for doubt.

Even the revisionists, except for a very few, concede that the bones are probably those of the princes. For one thing, the eyewitness description of their unearthing mentioned "rag and velvet." Velvet was not made until the 1400s, in Italy, and was so expensive in England that it was worn only by persons of the highest rank. "No other pair of boys of rank disappeared in the Tower between 1483 and 1674," wrote Alison Weir in her book on the princes. "To suggest otherwise is really to stretch coincidence too far."

All that is known for certain is that the princes entered the Tower in 1483 and shortly thereafter vanished from sight. Everything else is a mystery. The skeletons found in 1674 would seem to be those of Edward V and his brother, but there is no proof. Even if they are, there is no proof they were killed in 1483. As Kendall wrote,

The summary of these [scientific] findings and the circumstances under which the bones were discovered . . . indicate that the skeletons inurned in Westminster Abbey cannot be flatly and incontrovertibly identified as those of the sons of Edward IV.

Struggle for a King

The fates of young Edward V and his brother after they entered the Tower of London remain a mystery. The events that led to their imprisonment and eventual disappearance, however, were well documented at the time. The story is one of a tug-of-war between a dead king's brother on one side and his wife and her family on the other. The young princes were in the middle—along with the throne of England.

When Edward IV died in London on April 9, 1483, his older son, Edward, was at Ludlow Castle far to the west. Ludlow had long been a favorite residence of the members of the house of York. It was there in 1473 that the official household of Edward, Prince of Wales—the traditional title of the heir to the throne—had been established.

The ruins of Ludlow Castle. The castle belonged to the house of York and was where Prince Edward, son of Edward IV, first heard that his father, king of England, had died.

The Secret Marriage

In 1461, after King Edward IV defeated the Lancastrians at the Battle of Towton, it appeared the Wars of the Roses were over. It was Edward's rash marriage to Elizabeth Woodville that would prolong the conflict.

The story goes that Edward, while returning from Towton, was hunting in the woods near the town of Stony Stratford when he saw a beautiful woman holding two small boys by the hand. She knelt by his horse, looked up, and tearfully begged him to have mercy on her family. The woman was Elizabeth Woodville, whose husband, Lancastrian knight John Grey, had been killed in battle and had left her with two small sons.

Edward was overwhelmed by Elizabeth's beauty and tried to add her to his growing list of mistresses. Elizabeth, however, refused to submit to the king's advances. It was marriage or nothing.

Finally, Edward gave in. On May 1 at Grafton, home of Elizabeth's mother, he and Elizabeth were married. The only witnesses were Elizabeth's mother, two of her serving women, the priest, and a choirboy.

This marriage to a woman not of noble birth enraged Edward's strongest supporter, the earl of Warwick, who later joined forces with the Lancastrians and succeeded in forcing the king to flee from the country. It was during this time that Elizabeth sought sanctuary in Westminster Abbey, and it was there that her son, the future Edward V, was born.

The members of Elizabeth's large family were given high offices and titles by Edward IV. This aroused the jealousy of the more traditional nobility, and the Woodvilles' unpopularity eventually made it easier for Edward IV's brother Richard to overcome them after Edward's death.

The young prince had his own council and staff. Earl Rivers—Anthony Woodville, the queen's brother—was appointed Edward's governor and was in charge of the household. Two other brothers were on the council, as was Sir Richard Grey, the queen's son by her first husband, the late Sir John Grey, and her cousin, Sir Richard Haute. Yet another brother, Lionel Woodville, was chaplain. The prince's chamberlain, who had charge of his day-to-day needs such as clothing and food and had carried him in state processions before he could walk, was Sir Thomas Vaughan, another of the queen's relatives.

Thomas More wrote that the Woodvilles deliberately surrounded Edward with members of his mother's family so that "her blood might of youth be rooted in the Prince's favour." They wanted to ensure that Edward, when he came to the throne, would look first to them for advice and support.

Edward IV

Edward IV was famous for his free and easy lifestyle, but he laid down strict rules for his son. The prince was to "arise every morning at a convenient [suitable] time, and till he be made ready, none but Earl Rivers, his chamberlain and chaplain to enter his chamber, and one other chaplain to sing matins and then go to his chapel or chamber to hear mass." Each night, he was to "be in his chamber and for all night, and the traverse [curtain] drawn across by eight of the clock."

A Little-Known Prince

Much less is known about the younger prince, Richard, duke of York. He was brought up at the royal court in London by his mother. In 1478, when he was four years old, he was married to Anne Mowbray, duchess of Norfolk. Anne was only six at the time of the marriage, and she died in 1481. The only clue to Richard's personality comes from the French historian Jean Molinet, who wrote early in the next century that the boy "was joyous and witty, nimble, and ever ready for dances and games."

In a will written in 1475, Edward IV had entrusted the care of the princes to "our dearest wife the Queen." On his deathbed, however, he changed his mind, naming his brother Richard, duke of Gloucester, to be the young king's "protector," meaning that Gloucester would officially be in charge of Edward V.

England had had boy kings, but there was no established age at which they were supposed to be able to rule on their own. Edward III had taken control by force when he was seventeen. Richard II had been twenty-three when he declared himself of age. Edward V was only twelve in the spring of 1483, and the Woodvilles were afraid that Gloucester, if given the opportunity to rule, would take all power for himself and shut out the queen's family.

When Edward IV named Gloucester protector, the Woodvilles were shocked. They immediately took steps to thwart the late king's wishes and to gain power for themselves. Fortunately for them, Gloucester was far away at his castle of Middleham in northern England. Edward IV had made Gloucester his chief officer in the north, and Gloucester had remained there, spending very little time in London.

First, the Woodvilles took control of the royal treasury. An Italian observer, Dominic Mancini, wrote that Edward IV's fortune, "which had taken such years and such pains to gather, was divided between the queen mother [Elizabeth Woodville], the marquess [Thomas Grey, marquess of Dorset, the queen's other son by her first marriage] and Edward [Woodville, another of the queen's brothers]." Edward Woodville was named commander of the Royal Navy and took some of the treasure to sea. Dorset was deputy constable of the Tower of London and kept part of the treasure there, while Elizabeth, the dowager queen, took the rest. (When a British monarch dies and the crown passes to one of his children, his widow is formally referred to as the dowager queen, or simply "the queen.")

Elizabeth Is Refused

Next, Elizabeth confronted the royal council, which was meeting to decide how the kingdom would be governed. The dowager queen demanded to be named regent—the person who would rule in Edward V's name—but the council refused to go that far. The council then considered two options. The first was simply to honor Edward IV's deathbed wish and clear the way for Gloucester to govern. The second was for the council to govern in Edward V's name; this way, Gloucester would be the chief of the council but would not have absolute control. The queen's supporters, who had a majority on the council, voted for the second option.

By now, the Woodvilles had discovered that, by custom, the office of protector ended when a young monarch was formally crowned. After the coronation, a new royal council—which the Woodvilles hoped to dominate—would select the regent. Their new strategy became to have the young king crowned so quickly that Gloucester's protectorate would last, at most, only a few days. Indeed, they probably hoped that they could get Edward V crowned before Gloucester could learn of his brother's death and reach London.

Although the Woodvilles had made no attempt to inform Gloucester of his brother's death, they had sent a letter to Earl Rivers at Ludlow, telling him to bring the new king to London. They wanted Edward V secure in the capital, surrounded by the queen's family. They then sought to have the coronation as early as possible. Dorset was able to convince the council on April 11 to set a date of May 4, only three weeks away. Gloucester's supporters protested. They said such a decision should not be made without Gloucester present. Dorset, however, said, "We [the Woodvilles] are so important, that even without the king's uncle we can make and enforce these decisions."

Gloucester's strongest supporter on the council was William, Lord Hastings, who had been Edward IV's closest companion. Hastings, Mancini wrote, "was hostile to the entire kin of the

Elizabeth Woodville, queen of Edward IV, tried to circumvent her husband's wishes that Richard, duke of Gloucester, be in control of Edward V, her son.

Shakespeare's Richard

In his play *Richard III*, William Shakespeare did not attempt to show anything positive about Richard. Instead, Shakespeare's Richard is totally evil and makes that clear from the very first speech in the play.

The play opens after Edward IV has won his great victories at Barnet and Tewkesbury. Richard is in no mood to celebrate. As he, a hunchback, watches his brother—tall, handsome, adored by women—he says enviously:

> But I, that am not shaped for sportive tricks,
> Nor made to court an amorous looking-glass;
> I, that am rudely stamp'd, and want [lack] love's
>   majesty
> To strut before a wanton nymph . . .
> Cheated of feature by dissembling nature,
> Deform'd, unfinish'd, sent before my time
> Into this breathing world, scarce half made up . . .
> And therefore, since I cannot prove a lover,
> To entertain these fair well-spoken days,
> I am determinéd to prove a villain
> And hate the idle pleasures of these days.
> Plots have I laid, inductions dangerous . . .

Later, after he orders the execution of Rivers, Grey, and Vaughan, Richard says:

> But then I sigh; and, with a piece of scripture,
> Tell them that God bids us do good for evil:
> And thus I clothe my naked villainy
> With old odd ends stolen out of holy writ [scripture];
> And seem a saint, when most I play the devil.

The harshest description of Richard in the play comes from Margaret of Anjou, widow of Henry VI, who tells Richard's mother:

> From forth the kennel of thy womb hath crept
> A hell-hound that doth hunt us all to death:
> That dog, that had his teeth before his eyes,
> To worry [attack] lambs and lap their gentle blood,
> That foul defacer of God's handiwork,
> That excellent grand tyrant of the earth,
> That reigns in galléd [irritated] eyes of weeping souls,
> Thy womb let loose, to chase us to our graves.

Queen, on account of the Marquess of Dorset." Hastings and Dorset had quarreled over the late king's mistress, Elizabeth Shore, whom Edward had shared with Dorset but who, after the king's death, transferred her affections to Hastings.

A Loyal Friend

Hastings not only hated the Woodvilles, but he was also loyal to the memory of Edward IV and wanted the late king's wishes carried out. Once he saw that the Woodvilles meant to take power, and when he learned that no one had informed Gloucester of Edward IV's death, he sent a messenger to Gloucester advising him that his brother had died and he had been named protector. Mancini wrote that Hastings also urged Gloucester

> to hasten to the capital [London] with a strong force and avenge the insult done him by his enemies. He might easily obtain his revenge if, before reaching the city, he took the young King Edward under his protection and authority while seizing before they were alive to [aware of] the danger those of the king's followers, who were not in agreement with this policy [that Gloucester should be protector].

In addition, Hastings was able to limit the size of the armed force accompanying Edward V from Ludlow. The queen wanted Rivers to bring all the troops at his command, but Hastings realized that this would give the Woodvilles an army large enough to enforce their demands. He said that unless the escort was limited to two thousand troops, he would withdraw to Calais—the port city in France then held by England—of which he was governor. The queen knew that Hastings, once in Calais, could raise an army as large as hers. She backed down and agreed to limit the escort.

Gloucester, when he received Hastings's message, wrote a letter to the council in which, according to Mancini, he said that

> he had been loyal to his brother Edward . . . and would be, if only permitted, equally loyal to his brother's son, and to all his brother's issue [children], even female, if perchance, which God forbid, the youth should die. . . . This letter had a great effect on the minds of the people, who, as they had previously favoured the duke [Gloucester] in their hearts from a belief in his probity [integrity], now began to support him openly and aloud.

Planning a Meeting

Gloucester also wrote to Rivers at Ludlow. He pledged his loyalty to Edward V and asked what route Rivers planned to take from Ludlow to London. He wanted, he said, to be able to join the party and be with Edward as he entered his capital. Rivers replied that he and his people expected to be in Northampton by April 29 and that Gloucester could meet them there.

Gloucester had received another letter while at Middleham. This one was from Henry Stafford, duke of Buckingham. Buckingham, like Hastings, hated the Woodvilles. He was of noble blood, being descended from two sons of Edward III, but had been forced to marry Katherine Woodville, one of the queen's sisters, whom he "scorned to wed on account of her humble origin." Buckingham, who apparently knew of the Woodvilles' plan, offered to meet Gloucester and bring a thousand men with him. Gloucester wrote back that he would be happy to have Buckingham join him at

Henry Stafford

Northampton, but only to bring three hundred men—the same number Gloucester was bringing.

Even though the letter asking that the king be brought to London reached Ludlow on April 14, Rivers did not depart until April 24. He felt no urgency. Even Gloucester's letter aroused no suspicions. Otherwise, Rivers never would have agreed for the two parties to meet at Northampton. The queen, however, was afraid of what Gloucester might do. She sent her son Sir Richard Grey to find Rivers and to tell him to come as quickly as possible.

Rivers and the king were met by Grey at Northampton on April 29. Rivers, now suspicious of Gloucester, did not stop at Northampton, but took the king fourteen miles down the road toward London to the town of Stony Stratford. He left young Edward at an inn there and then, with Grey and a small escort of soldiers, rode back to Northampton to meet Gloucester. Why he did so is not known. According to one chronicle of the time, Rivers thought he could persuade Gloucester to accept the council's decision. It is also possible that, having accepted Gloucester's invitation to meet, he could not refuse to do so without showing open hostility and perhaps provoking Gloucester to take action. Whatever Rivers's reason for leaving, he told the commander of the king's escort to depart for London early the next morning even if he himself had not returned.

A Jolly Dinner

When Rivers reached Northampton, Gloucester was already there. Rivers explained the absence of the king by saying that Northampton lacked sufficient space to house the escorts of the king, Gloucester, and Buckingham. Gloucester, seemingly in a friendly mood, readily accepted this excuse and asked Rivers to have dinner with him at the inn where they were to stay. As the two noblemen were dining, Buckingham arrived and joined them. It was a jolly meal, as More wrote, with "much friendly cheer between these dukes and the Lord Ryvers a great while."

Late in the evening, Rivers went off to bed. Once he had left, the jovial mood disappeared. Gloucester, Buckingham, and their closest advisers, according to More, "set them down in council, wherein they spent most of the night." Like his late brother Edward IV, Gloucester was capable of swift action. The two dukes decided that they must take possession of the king and that this was their best—and perhaps only—opportunity.

The dukes took over the keys to the inn, woke their servants, and instructed them to be ready to ride at dawn. Rivers's servants were allowed to sleep undisturbed. Armed men were sent to guard the road between Northampton and Stony Stratford so that no message could be sent to the king.

When Rivers awoke, he found himself locked inside the inn and "marvellously misliked so great a change in so few hours." When he demanded to know the reason, Gloucester and Buckingham accused him of attempting "to set distance between the king and them and bring them to confusion." Rivers began to protest and was arrested.

Gloucester and Buckingham then set out for Stony Stratford. With them, they took Grey who apparently had not been at the dinner the night before. When they arrived, they found that King Edward and his escort had mounted their horses and were about to set out for London. The dukes approached the king with every sign of loyalty. The *Croyland Chronicle*—so called because it was written shortly afterward at Croyland Abbey—said that Gloucester

Richard forces his nephew Edward V from the protection of Lord Rivers. In order to make sure nothing stood in his way of the crown, however, Richard had to also get control of Edward's brother, Richard.

"did not refuse to pay every mark of respect to the King his nephew, in the way of uncovering his head, bending the knee or other posture required of a subject."

Laying the Blame

Gloucester began by expressing his sympathy to the boy for the recent death of his father. He then went on to blame the late king's death on the Woodvilles, who he said were "the servants and companions of his [Edward IV's] vices, and had ruined his health." They must be removed, Gloucester said, before they could bring harm to the new king. Furthermore, he charged the Woodvilles with plotting to kill him and deprive him of the lawful role of protector given him by Edward IV.

Richard's Other Victims

The princes in the Tower are by no means the only people King Richard III is alleged to have killed. Although there has never been proof, some historians have accused Richard of claiming many more victims, including one of his brothers and his wife.

One story said that after the Battle of Tewkesbury, Prince Edward, son of King Henry VI, was brought before Edward IV. Asked a question by King Edward, the prince made a bold reply and was supposedly stabbed to death by Richard and his brother George, duke of Clarence.

Richard's next victim is supposed to have been King Henry VI. After Tewkesbury, Edward IV returned to London in triumph and his predecessor, the dim-witted Henry, was put in the Tower. Shortly thereafter, it was announced that Henry was dead. Richard was known to have been in the Tower at the time, and some historians think he supervised, on Edward's orders, the murder of Henry.

According to Shakespeare, Richard brought about the execution of his brother, the duke of Clarence, who supposedly was drowned in a barrel of his favorite wine. No shred of evidence exists to support this claim. In fact, Richard was living far to the north at the time of Clarence's death, protested the execution strongly, and accused the Woodvilles of bringing it about.

Richard's last victim is supposed to have been his queen, Anne. At the time of Anne's death in 1485, it was rumored that Richard had fallen in love with his niece Elizabeth Woodville and had poisoned his wife to get her out of the way. By this time, most people in England believed Richard had murdered his nephews and were willing to believe any evil of him, regardless of whether there was any proof.

Prince Edward of Wales (left) is about to be killed by order of King Edward IV of England in the Battle of Tewkesbury.

Grey started to protest, but Buckingham harshly ordered him to be quiet. The king, hearing Gloucester's accusations, replied, "What my brother [Dorset] has done I cannot say, but in good faith I dare well answer for my Lord Rivers, and my brother here [Grey], that they be innocent of any such matter."

Buckingham interrupted, saying, "They have the dealing of these matters far from the knowledge of your good Grace."

Edward, showing remarkable courage for a boy of twelve, pressed on. Mancini wrote that he said that "as for the government, he had great confidence in the peers of the realm and the Queen." Buckingham again interrupted, bluntly telling the king that "it was not the business of women but of men to rule Kingdoms."

The two dukes arrested Grey, Sir Thomas Vaughan, and Sir Richard Haute and had them taken away. Edward saw that further protest would be of no use. Mancini wrote that the king "surrendered himself to the care of his uncle, which was inevitable, for although the dukes cajoled [charmed] him by moderation, yet they clearly showed that they were demanding rather than supplicating [pleading]."

Gloucester dismissed the soldiers who had been escorting Edward, telling them not to "approach any place to which the King might chance to come, under penalty of death." Their leaders having been arrested, the soldiers obeyed meekly. Gloucester and Buckingham then took Edward back to Northampton where they replaced his personal servants with their own men. At last, the young king's courage faltered. He "wept and was nothing content, but it booted [helped him] not."

A Celebration

The victorious dukes then sat down to another meal, this one a celebration. Gloucester was in such a good mood that he had a dish from his own table sent to Rivers, "praying him to be of good cheer, all should be well enough." Rivers politely declined, asking that the food be taken instead to Grey, who he said had more need of comfort.

Later in the day, Mancini says, Gloucester wrote to the royal council and the mayor of London, assuring them that

he had not confined his nephew the King of England, rather had he rescued him and the realm from perdition

[ruin], since the young man would have fallen into the hands of those who, since they had not spared either the honour or the life of the father, could not be expected to have more regard for the youthfulness of the son. No-one, save only him [Gloucester], had such solicitude [concern] for the welfare of King Edward and the preservation of the state. At an early date, he and the boy would come to the City [London] so that the coronation might be more splendidly performed.

There is nothing to indicate that Gloucester was telling anything but the truth and that he did intend to govern England in the king's name. If his plan all along had been to murder his nephew, he could have done it more easily at Northampton than later, in London. On the other hand, he would have gained little by killing Edward at this time while the king's younger brother was alive and protected by the Woodvilles. Things had happened so quickly that Gloucester probably had not thought much about what to do next. His first goal, however, that of gaining control of King Edward, had been accomplished.

Into the Tower

When Richard of Gloucester seized control of King Edward V on April 30 in Northampton, he had taken the first step toward seizing the crown itself. It is not certain whether this was his goal all along, as both More and Mancini later claimed. The events of the next six weeks, however, would fix the course of Gloucester and his nephews alike—Gloucester to the throne and the young princes to the Tower.

Richard and the duke of Buckingham had intercepted the king and placed his Woodville attendants under arrest early in the morning. By midnight, the news of what they had done reached London. It was greeted very differently by different people.

Hastings, who had first warned Gloucester about what the Woodvilles were up to, was elated. In other parts of London, wrote More, there was "great commotion and murmur." And Mancini claimed that "there was current in the capital a sinister rumour that the duke [Gloucester] had brought his nephew not under his care, but into his power, so as to gain for himself the crown." Hastings read Gloucester's letters aloud, first to an assembly of noblemen and then to the ordinary citizens. So great was Hastings's popularity and the people's faith in his loyalty to Edward IV's son that "all praised the duke of Gloucester for his dutifulness to his nephews and for his intention to punish their enemies."

For the queen and the other Woodvilles in London, the news meant the ruin of their dreams of power. At first, they considered trying to meet Gloucester with force. During the early hours of May 1, Dorset tried to raise troops from some nobles he thought might support him. He was met, not only with refusal, but also with open hostility. The Woodvilles were very unpopular with the rest of the nobility, who considered them upstarts and had resented the wealth and honors given to them by Edward IV.

Elizabeth Woodville had not waited to see what would come of Dorset's efforts. Her son Edward had been taken by her enemies. And another son, Richard Grey, and Lord Rivers, her brother, had been "sent no man wist [knew] whither, to be done with God wot what [God only knew]." Once more, as she had done in 1470, she fled, seeking sanctuary in Westminster Abbey. With her went her five daughters and her remaining son, Richard, duke of York. Ironically, it was the nineteenth anniversary of her wedding to Edward IV.

Arrival in Haste

Elizabeth took refuge, not in the sanctuary building on the abbey grounds, along with debtors and common criminals, but in the house of the abbot himself. She was not in such a hurry, however,

Upon hearing the news that Gloucester had taken her son, Elizabeth Woodville fled, seeking sanctuary at Westminster Abbey (pictured).

that she was willing to leave her possessions behind. The next morning, wrote More, the scene at the abbey was one of

> much heaviness, rumble, haste, and business—carriage
> [carrying] and conveyance of her stuff into sanctuary,
> chests, coffers [boxes], packs, fardels [parcels], trusses
> [bundles] all on men's backs, no man unoccupied, some
> lading [loading], some discharging [unloading], some
> coming for more, some breaking down the walls to bring in
> the next [nearest] way. The queen herself sat alone, alow
> [low] on the rushes, all desolate and dismayed.

When a message was brought to Elizabeth from Hastings, assuring her that all would be well, she burst out, "Ah, woe worth him [be to him]! For he is one of them that laboureth to destroy me and my blood [family]." Later in the day, she was joined in sanctuary by her son Dorset, who had given up trying to raise troops. He brought with him his share of Edward IV's treasure from the Tower.

Hastings sent a messenger to Northampton to tell Gloucester what had happened in London. Gloucester, knowing it was safe to proceed, wrote back that he and the king would enter London on May 4. Before he left Northampton, however, Gloucester sent Rivers, Grey, and Vaughan to separate castles in the north to be held prisoners.

Gloucester, Buckingham, and King Edward set out for London on the morning of May 3 with about five hundred soldiers. They spent that night in the town of Saint Albans, about twenty-five miles north of the capital. The two dukes apparently made some effort to win the confidence of the king. At one point in the evening, the three signed their names to a piece of parchment, now on display in the British Museum. Across the top is written, in bold letters, "Edwardus Quintus." Below, in fine, precise writing, is the signature of "Richard Gloucestre" with his motto "Loyaulté me lie" [loyalty binds me]. At the bottom is scrawled "Souvene me souvene [think of me often] Harre Bokynham."

A Royal Entry

The next day, the king and dukes were met north of London by the mayor and city officials, all wearing red robes, and more than four hundred members of the livery companies—trade organizations—dressed in violet. After an official welcome, the young king, dressed

This depiction of Elizabeth Woodville makes her appear placid and devout. From what is known about her, however, she and her family were not averse to using whatever powers necessary to use Edward to take control of the throne.

in blue velvet, rode into the city. On either side, in black (to symbolize mourning for Edward IV, were Gloucester and Buckingham. Crowds of people lined the streets to cheer, and Gloucester bowed low in his saddle and shouted to them, "Behold your prince and sovereign lord."

Gloucester was trying to convince the people of his loyalty to Edward. He also wasted no time trying to convince them that the Woodvilles had been out to kill him and intended to rule by force. Ahead of the procession were four wagons loaded with weapons and armor in barrels bearing the Woodville crest. Gloucester's men shouted to the people that the weapons had been found stored along the road, proof that the Woodvilles had been preparing to ambush Gloucester as he came to London. Many people believed this, not stopping to wonder why, if an ambush was planned, the weapons had been found nailed up in barrels rather than in the hands of Woodville troops. According to Mancini, many others would have known that Edward IV had placed weapons at convenient points north of London in case an army had to march quickly against Scotland.

The procession ended at the palace of the bishop of London, where the king was to be temporarily housed. In the palace courtyard, Gloucester assembled the leading nobles, citizens, and church officials and had them swear loyalty to Edward. This was done "by all with the greatest pleasure and delight," said the *Croyland Chronicle*, which added that Hastings "was bursting with joy at the way things were turning out."

There is no record of what King Edward thought of all this pomp and ceremony. It should have been one of the happiest days of his life, but it was probably saddened by the lack of familiar faces. Where was his mother? Where was his uncle Rivers? Where was his brother Richard? He was installed in the palace with servants to see to every need, but they were Gloucester's men, not those with whom he was familiar.

The New Council

On May 10 a new royal council met. Some of the members— Hastings, Lord Thomas Stanley, Archbishop Thomas Rotherham, Bishop Robert Stillington, and Bishop John Morton—were primarily loyal to the memory of Edward IV and, therefore, to his son. Others—Buckingham, Lord John Howard, and Viscount Francis Lovell—were strong supporters of Gloucester. Others had no strong ties one way or another, like Archbishop Thomas Bourchier and Bishop John Russell, thought by many historians to be the author of the *Croyland Chronicle*. One newcomer, who would play a major role later, was William Catesby, a lawyer in Hastings's service, whom Richard put on the council at Hastings's request.

Although this council met at the bishop's palace, there is no record that King Edward was present. The first order of business was to formally grant Gloucester the title of protector. By this act, he received custody of the king and full powers to govern in the king's name until the coronation, which was moved to a new date, June 22. Parliament—England's lawmaking assembly—was called for June 25. At that time, a council of regency was to be established to rule in Edward's name until he came of age. The council presumably would be headed by Gloucester.

Next, the council discussed where Edward was to live
coronation, the bishop's palace being considered unsui
logical place, Westminster Palace, was considered too
Westminster Abbey, where the queen and Edward's bro
sisters remained. Finally, Buckingham suggested the Tow
don and, after some discussion, all agreed. No one consid
site to be threatening. It was not until the next century
Tower gained a reputation as primarily a prison.

Thus far, Gloucester had had his way. However, when h
convince the council to condemn Rivers, Grey, Ha
Vaughan for treason, he failed. The council argued that
definition of treason was an attempt to take the life of the
queen, or the heir to the throne. Rivers had done none

*Gloucester decided to place Edward V in the Tower of London (p.
This did not arouse suspicions because the tower was not used p
as a prison at that time.*

urthermore, it said, even if the assassination of the protector were treason, Gloucester had not been formally named protector when, he claimed, Rivers planned to kill him. The majority of the council went even further, expressing concern that "the Protector did not, with a sufficient degree of considerateness, take fitting care for the preservation of the dignity and safety of the Queen."

A Setback for Gloucester

The failure of the council to condemn the Woodvilles was a major setback for Gloucester. If he did, indeed, plan on nothing more than ruling England through his nephew, he would have a struggle for power with Elizabeth and her family—a struggle he might well lose. Once Edward was crowned, the young king probably would do everything he could to restore the Woodvilles to power. It may have been this likelihood that finally led Gloucester to take the throne for himself.

Sometime between May 10 and May 19, King Edward and his household were transferred to the Tower. This much is known because a grant exists dated May 19, 1483, issued by Edward "at our Tower of London." He lived in the royal apartments that had been built along the south wall of the White Tower, the same apartments that were demolished in 1674. He was by no means a prisoner, but rather was surrounded by a small court. Papers were brought for him to sign, many of them worded "by thadvise [the advice] of oure derrest Oncle the duc of Gloucestre protector and defensor of this our Royaume [realm] during our yong Age."

Everything appeared normal except for one thing. To Gloucester's embarrassment, the queen refused to emerge from sanctuary or to allow her children to be taken from her. Members of the council—both those who had served her husband and those supporting Gloucester—tried to convince her that no harm would come to her family, but Elizabeth Woodville refused to emerge from the safety of Westminster Abbey.

The council's refusal to condemn the Woodvilles for treason did not stop Gloucester from seizing their lands and property, although he had no legal right to do so. He transferred much of this property and the offices held by the Woodvilles to his own supporters. Buckingham received huge grants of land and was named Chief Justice of England. Howard and Catesby were well rewarded.

Hastings, however, received only an appointment as Master of the Mint—where money was coined—and was reaffirmed in his offices of lord chamberlain and captain of Calais. This comparatively small reward may have indicated that Gloucester resented that Hastings was loyal to Edward V, not to him.

Richard's Deformity

According to William Shakespeare, King Richard III was a "poisonous, hunch-backed toad," twisted both in body and mind. This has been the traditional picture of Richard—an evil man whose inner nature was mirrored in outward deformity.

Actually, there were no references during Richard's lifetime to any physical disability. To be sure, he was not a typical member of the Plantagenet family—tall and blond. Rather, he was short and dark like his father, the duke of York. A sixteenth-century historian, John Stow, reported talking with men who had known Richard and who reported him to be "of bodily shape comely [shapely] enough, only of low stature."

Reports of disability began only after Richard's death at Bosworth. In the days of the next king, Henry VII, Sir Thomas More, Polydore Vergil, and John Rous all mentioned that one of Richard's shoulders was higher than the other, but they disagreed on which shoulder.

Many people in the Middle Ages believed physical deformity was a sign of an evil mind. It was possibly for that reason that later historians, unfriendly to Richard, exaggerated what perhaps was only a slight inequality in the shoulders. More, for instance, referred to Richard baring his "shriveled withered arm."

The earliest known drawings and paintings of Richard show no deformity. One portrait, dating from about 1520, did depict Richard as a hunchback, but X rays revealed that the deformity had been painted into the original canvas years later.

Certainly, whatever physical disability Richard had, it was small. His ability on the battlefield was well known. A person as deformed as Shakespeare's Richard could not have fought so spectacularly in the Battle of Bosworth, where the king struck down the famous Sir John Cheney, said to be a giant.

Hastings Is Suspicious

By the last week in May, Hastings and the others on the council who were loyal to Edward had become suspicious of Gloucester. They knew, for instance, that he wanted to extend his term as protector beyond the coronation. Bishop Russell had begun to write a speech with which to open Parliament on June 25. In it, he would argue that the safety of England depended on Gloucester's acting as protector until Edward came of age at fifteen. Hastings and the others suspected that Gloucester's real intention was to become king.

By June, the council was divided. Those supporting Gloucester, including Buckingham and Howard, were meeting privately. Those loyal to King Edward—including Hastings, Stanley, Morton, and Rotherham—met secretly in one another's houses. Each group was trying to discover what the other was doing. Stanley warned Hastings that such a division of the council was dangerous. "For while we talk of one matter in the one place," Stanley said, "little know we whereof they talk in the other place." Hastings told Stanley not to worry. His man Catesby, who was meeting with Gloucester's group, would keep Hastings informed. Little did he know that Catesby was now firmly on Gloucester's side and was reporting all Hastings did to the protector.

Although Gloucester suspected Hastings of plotting against him, Hastings was still popular with the nobility and with the citizens of London. Gloucester wanted Hastings on his side and sent someone—More says it was Catesby, and Mancini says it was Buckingham—to see whether Hastings would accept Gloucester as king. More wrote that Catesby "found him [Hastings] so steadfast [in his loyalty to Edward] and heard him speak so terrible words that he durst [dared] no further proceed."

Gloucester knew that without Hastings's support he could not hope to win the backing of the others on the council who were loyal to King Edward. He decided to get rid of them by force. On June 10 he wrote a letter to the council of the city of York asking the people there

> to come unto us in London, in all the diligence ye can possible after the sight hereof [the letter], with as many as ye can defensibly arrayed [gathered], there to aid and assist us against the Queen, her blood adherents [family] and affinity

42

[followers], which have intended, and daily doth intend, to murder and utterly destroy us and our cousin the Duke of Buckingham and the old royal blood of this realm.

Richard also wrote letters asking Henry Percy, earl of Northumberland, and Lord Ralph Neville to raise troops. Catesby carried these letters north on Gloucester's behalf. He also carried warrants ordering the execution of Rivers, Vaughan, Haute, and Grey "so as to leave no source of danger to himself from any quarter."

Gloucester's Trap

Gloucester carefully set a trap for Hastings and the other councilors opposed to him. He called a special meeting for part of the council at the Tower; this group included Buckingham, Hastings, Morton, Stanley, Rotherham, and Howard. The other councilors were instructed to meet at Westminster to review plans for the coronation.

The story of the meeting at the Tower, on June 13, comes from More, who probably heard it from Morton, in whose household the future statesman served as a child. At first, Gloucester appeared in a good mood. He apologized for being an hour late, then asked Morton if he had any more of the strawberries for which his garden was famous. Morton hastened to send a servant to fetch the berries. Gloucester left the room, leaving the councilors to discuss routine business. When he returned, More wrote, he was "all changed, with a wonderfully sour angry countenance, knitting the brows, frowning, and fretting and gnawing on his lips."

Finally, Gloucester asked Hastings what punishment was deserved by those "who conspire against the life of one so nearly related to the king as myself, and entrusted with the government of the realm?"

Confused, Hastings replied, "Certainly if they have so heinously done they are worth a heinous punishment."

"What!" shouted Gloucester. "Dost thou serve me with 'ifs' and 'ands'? I tell thee they [the Woodvilles] have done it, and that I will make good upon thy body, traitor!"

The protector went on to accuse Hastings and other councilors of plotting with Elizabeth Woodville to kill him. He said they had used Elizabeth Shore, Edward IV's former mistress, to carry messages back and forth. He claimed "yonder witch" [Shore] had used sorcery against him. He supposedly pulled up his sleeve to show that the arm had withered.

43

More was probably exaggerating. By the time he was writing—about 1515—stories had grown up that Gloucester had had various obvious deformities. William Shakespeare portrayed him as a hunchback in the play *Richard III*. Actually, there is no evidence that Gloucester was deformed, although one shoulder apparently was slightly higher than the other. Indeed, if he had been nearly as deformed as later writers claimed, he would not have been able to perform in battle as capably as he did when he fought in the Wars of the Roses.

The Death of Hastings

Upon finishing his speech, Gloucester banged his fist on the table. This was his signal for armed men, who had been waiting outside, to burst into the room, shouting, "Treason!" In the scuffle, Stanley was wounded. Hastings, Rotherham, and Morton were seized. Stanley, Rotherham, and Morton were taken away, but Gloucester told Hastings he had better say his prayers "for, by St. Paul, I will not [go] to dinner until I see thy head off."

In the play Richard III, *Shakespeare depicts Richard as having a severe hunchback. Historians believe that Shakespeare's portrayal is historically inaccurate, added to make Richard seem more evil.*

Hastings was dragged from the chamber and onto the grounds of the Tower. Evidently, some sort of construction was under way, and a large, square wooden beam lay on the ground. Hastings was not even given a chance to make his confession to a priest. His head was forced down onto the beam and hacked off by a sword. "Thus fell Hastings," wrote Mancini, "killed not by those enemies he had always feared, but by a friend whom he had never doubted." Although no one knows, it is very possible that the young king heard the commotion and, from a window, was able to see the death of his father's greatest friend.

Polydore Vergil, an Italian historian commissioned in the next century by Henry VII to write a history of England, reports that Gloucester then sent his own men running through the streets of London crying "Treason! Treason!" The Londoners, alarmed, began seizing weapons and running toward the Tower. They were met by Gloucester and Buckingham, wearing rusty armor. This armor was all they had time to put on, they claimed, when they had discovered that Hastings had meant to murder them at the council meeting. Gloucester also sent messengers throughout London to read a lengthy proclamation outlining Hastings's supposed crimes. More wrote, however, that even "every child might well perceive that it [the proclamation] had been prepared before [the council meeting]."

The Second Prince

With the death of Hastings and the arrest of Stanley, Rotherham, and Morton, there was no opposition on the council to Gloucester's becoming king. Only one step remained. He had to get King Edward's brother, the young duke of York, into his custody. He was afraid that even if he declared himself king, Edward IV's younger son might escape him and become the center of opposition.

Vergil wrote that in a council meeting on June 16, Gloucester, still claiming that Edward would be crowned, said, "What a sight it shall [would] be to see the King crowned if, while that the solemnity of triumphant pomp is in doing, his mother, brother, and sisters remain in sanctuary." He claimed that the prince was being held by his mother against his will and that the king was lonely and missed his young brother. Besides, he said, such a young child could not possibly be guilty of any crime and could not legally seek sanctuary.

At last, he convinced the council to send Archbishop Bourchier and Howard to Westminster Abbey to try to convince the dowager queen to relinquish her youngest son. They did not go alone. The *Croyland Chronicle* says that Gloucester went "with a great multitude to Westminster . . . armed with swords and staves [staffs]." Mancini says the abbey was "surrounded with troops." Clearly, the message was that if Elizabeth did not surrender her son, he would be taken by force.

Bourchier and Howard tried to convince the queen that the young prince would come to no harm. She was doubtful, More wrote, because she knew there were "deadly enemies of my blood. The desire of a kingdom knoweth no kindred; brothers have been brother's bane [death], and may the nephew be sure of the uncle?"

Elizabeth Shore

When Richard III ordered the sudden execution of William, Lord Hastings, he charged him with plotting with Elizabeth Woodville, accusing the alleged conspirators of using Elizabeth Shore to carry messages back and forth.

Elizabeth Shore, sometimes mistakenly called "Jane," was the wife of a cloth dealer in London. In the early 1470s, she became one of the favorite mistresses of King Edward IV. Edward is known to have shared some of his mistresses with his friends, and Elizabeth was the lover of Edward's brother-in-law, the marquess of Dorset, while King Edward lived. After Edward's death, however, she left Dorset for Hastings.

After Hastings was beheaded, Richard ordered the bishop of London to punish Elizabeth Shore for her immorality. She was put in prison, but beforehand was made to walk through the streets of London to St. Paul's Cathedral wearing only her kirtle [a loose undergown] and carrying a lighted candle as a sign of repentance.

Sir Thomas More, who was too young to have witnessed this scene but knew Shore later in her life, wrote that she was "so fair and lovely" and blushed so modestly that she aroused the pity of the crowd—and in some men, the lust.

Shore was in prison only a short time. After her release, she married her lawyer, Thomas Lynom. She died, widowed and in poverty, in 1526.

With great misgivings, Elizabeth parts with her son Richard, placing him in the hands of the duke of Gloucester. She would never see him again.

At last, the archbishop pleaded with Elizabeth to release her son voluntarily, explaining that otherwise the boy would be taken by force, even though Gloucester "thought or intended no harm."

Finally, wrote Mancini, "When the Queen saw herself besieged and preparation for violence, she surrendered her son, trusting in the word of the Cardinal of Canterbury [Bourchier] that the boy should be restored after the coronation." More wrote that she told young Richard, "Farewell, my own sweet son. God send you good keeping. Let me kiss you once yet ere you go, for God knows when we shall kiss again." Then, she "wept and went her way, leaving the child weeping fast."

Richard, duke of York, was taken from Westminster Abbey to Westminster Palace where his uncle waited for him. There, wrote More, he was met by Gloucester, who "took him in his arms and kissed him with these words: 'Now welcome, my Lord, even with all my heart.' Thereupon, forthwith they brought him unto the King his brother . . . into the Tower, out of which, after that day, they never came abroad."

King Richard III

Once Richard, duke of Gloucester, had both his royal nephews under his control in the Tower of London, he moved quickly to strip young Edward V of his title and become king in his place. He had to move quickly. He had gotten Prince Richard out of Westminster Abbey on June 16. Now, less than a week remained until the scheduled coronation of Edward on June 22.

"From this day," said the *Croyland Chronicle,* "the Duke openly revealed his plans." He had already confided in Buckingham. Now, he also took Howard and Sir Edmund Shaa, mayor of London, into his confidence. The time was right for them to act "ere men could have time to devise any way to resist." The opposition on the council had been silenced. The citizens of London were confused, and no person "wist [knew] what to think nor whom to trust." Many of the great nobles of England, who might have provided opposition to Gloucester, were in London already for the upcoming coronation and "out of their own strengths." That is, they were away from their own castles and soldiers and were unable to resist a takeover.

On June 17, Gloucester issued orders canceling the Parliament that had been summoned. That same day, Edward V signed the last state paper that has survived bearing his name. Next, Gloucester postponed the coronation, on what excuse no one knows today. Up until now, he had appeared in public dressed in black, as if in mourning for his brother. Now, he rode through the London streets wearing a purple robe and was "surrounded by a thousand attendants."

Finally, Gloucester gained control of the last of his own family who could possibly be a contender for the crown. This was the son of his other dead brother, George, duke of Clarence. Gloucester ordered this nephew, the eight-year-old earl of Warwick, to be brought to London and imprisoned. Gloucester and his friends now lacked only one important thing—an excuse through which they could justify taking the throne away from Edward. English history was full of kings who had been deposed—Edward II, Richard II, and Henry VI—but it had been claimed that they were unfit to rule, guilty of bad government or of excessive generosity to royal favorites. Clearly, the twelve-year-old Edward could be charged with nothing like this.

A Shocking Sermon

Since he could not prove that his nephew had been a bad king, Gloucester had to try to prove that Edward had no right to be king in the first place. He arranged to have the well-known priest Ralph Shaa, the mayor's brother, preach a sermon on Sunday, June 22, stating Gloucester's claim to the throne. In those days—before newspapers or other mass media—most people got news by word of mouth, and the church pulpit was one of the best ways to spread propaganda. Shaa delivered his sermon to a good-size crowd at St. Paul's Cross, a large, open space next to St. Paul's Cathedral.

St. Paul's Cross, the large open area where Shaa cast doubt on Edward IV's claim to the crown.

The theme for the sermon was a sentence from the biblical Book of Wisdom: "But the multiplying brood of the ungodly shall not thrive, nor take rooting from bastard slips [grafts from a plant], nor lay any fast foundation." According to Vergil, Shaa claimed

> that the late king Edward was not begotten [fathered] by Richard duke of York but by some other, who privily [secretly] had had knowledge of [sexual relations with] his mother; and that the same did manifestly appear by sure demonstrations, because king Edward was neither in physnomy [facial features] nor shape of body like unto Richard the father; for he [King Edward] was high of stature, the other [the duke of York] very little; he of large face, the other, short and round.

At this point in the sermon, Gloucester was supposed to appear—as if by chance—on a nearby balcony where all could see how closely he resembled his late father. Shaa's timing was evidently off, because Gloucester failed to appear. The priest had already gone on to other subjects by the time the protector made his entrance. According to More, Shaa immediately broke off in midsentence and repeated what he had said earlier: "This is the very noble prince, the special pattern of knightly prowess, which as well in all princely behavior as in the lineaments [outlines] and features of his visage [face] represents the very face of the noble Duke of York his father."

Standing Like Stones

The plan had been that the crowd, swayed by Shaa's eloquence, would raise a great shout and proclaim Gloucester king. Instead, wrote More, they "stood as if they had been turned into stones." Vergil wrote that the people were shocked that Gloucester would allow the priest "to condemn, in open audience [in public], his mother of adultery, a woman of most pure and honorable life." Shaa's reputation was so damaged that he ceased to appear in public but "kept him out of sight like an owl."

Gloucester's mother, Cecily of York, who was highly respected by the public as a faithful wife and had taken vows as a nun after the death of her husband, was outraged. She "complained afterward in sundry places to right many noble men . . . of that great injury which her son Richard had done her." This reaction, plus the memory of the crowd's lack of response, caused Gloucester to backtrack and seek a new strategy. Since he could no longer argue that his brother Edward IV had been illegitimate, he would attempt to show that Edward's sons, now secure in the Tower, were illegitimate.

Gloucester determined to use a story told to him by Bishop Stillington. A French diplomat, Philippe de Commynes, writing in about 1490, claimed that Stillington had told the royal council on June 8 that King Edward IV had not been free to marry Elizabeth Woodville in 1464 because he had already entered into a premarriage contract with a woman named Eleanor Butler. The bishop said that he personally had conducted a ceremony that, although not a marriage, was just as binding according to church law. Stillington had waited so long to tell his story, he said, because he was afraid of the Woodvilles.

This time, Gloucester chose Buckingham to state his case. The leading citizens of London were called to the Guildhall—something like a city hall—along with all the noblemen who had come to the city for the coronation. There, on June 24, Buckingham gave a long, eloquent address. His speech was quoted at length by More, who probably heard details of it from his father, who—as a London judge—was probably there.

Buckingham's Speech at the Guildhall

Buckingham began by attacking the Woodvilles and then talked about the late king's morals, saying that "no woman was there anywhere . . . whom he set his eye upon, in whom he anything liked . . . but . . . he would importunately [resolutely] pursue his appetite and have her." He went on to say—according to More—that Ralph Shaa two days earlier had already told about Edward IV's pre-contract. More was probably mistaken about this, since none of the writers at the time mentioned it in connection with Shaa's sermon. Furthermore, More mistakenly identified the woman as Elizabeth Lucy, who had been one of Edward IV's many mistresses, rather than Eleanor Butler.

Buckingham passed quickly over the part of the story alleging Edward IV's illegitimacy, doing so—he said—out of respect for Gloucester, "who bears, as nature requires, a filial devotion to the Duchess [of York] his mother." Instead, he reminded his listeners of the passage in the Bible that says, "Woe to that realm that has a child to their King." Some of the leading nobles of England, he said, "not willing any bastard blood to have rule of the land," had prepared a petition (probably written by Gloucester, Buckingham, and Howard) asking Gloucester to become king.

Gloucester, said Buckingham, would be reluctant to take on such a burden, but might do so if the people implored him. "Wherein, dear friends," he said, "what mind you have, we request you plainly to show us."

To his amazement, Buckingham received the same reaction that had greeted Shaa two days earlier. Instead of crying out that Gloucester should be king, the people were silent. Buckingham asked the mayor of London, who stood nearby, what this meant. The mayor replied that perhaps the audience had not understood. Buckingham tried again, "somewhat louder," but the people were "as still as midnight."

Richard (seated) convinced Buckingham (left) to plead his case before the public that he should be king. Buckingham received a cold response.

Earl Rivers

The Woodvilles, relatives of Edward IV's queen, have usually been portrayed as grasping, greedy, and unscrupulous. And, in fact, most of them were. The exception seems to have been Elizabeth's brother Anthony Woodville, Earl Rivers, called by writer Giles St. Aubyn "the most attractive member of an unloved family." Although he was at the center of the Woodvilles' plans for power, Rivers seems to have been a patron of the arts, a gifted poet and scholar, and a deeply religious person.

Rivers was the chief patron of William Caxton, one of England's earliest printers. One book, thought to have been the first Caxton printed in England, was a religious work translated from the French by Rivers, who presented it to King Edward IV as a present. Rivers translated other books on religious themes, which Caxton printed. In addition to translating, Rivers wrote poems and ballads encouraging people to avoid the so-called seven deadly sins.

Outwardly, Rivers was a splendid courtier, as elegantly dressed as anyone. Under his fine clothes, however, he wore a shirt woven of rough hair to remind him of his vow.

Before he was executed at Pontefract Castle, Rivers wrote a poem in which he reflected philosophically on how he had come to his death. The last verse read:

> My life was lent
> Me to one intent.
> It is nigh spent.
> Welcome Fortune!
> But I ne went [never thought]
> Thus to be shent [ruined]
> But she it meant:
> Such is her won [custom].

In his will, Rivers made bequests, not only to his wife but also to hospitals, to religious houses, and to the poor. It is interesting that he left nothing, not even a keepsake, to his sister the queen.

At last, Buckingham tried a third time, saying, "Wherefore we require you give us answer one or other, whether you be minded, as all the nobles of this realm to be, to have this noble Prince, now Protector, to be your King, or not." The crowd began to murmur, sounding—wrote More—"like a swarm of bees." Finally, a small group of Buckingham's and Gloucester's men began to throw their caps in the air and shout "King Richard! King Richard!"

Seizing the Moment

Buckingham quickly seized his opportunity. He told the crowd:

> Wherefore, friends . . . since we perceive it is all your whole minds to have this noble man for your king—whereof we shall make his Grace [Gloucester] so effectual report that we doubt not but it shall redound [contribute] unto your great weal [wealth] and advantage—we request that you tomorrow go with us and we with you unto his noble Grace, to make our humble request unto him in the manner before rehearsed.

All this—the pre-contract charge and the acceptance of the petition—was highly illegal. Parliament had the authority to offer the crown to Gloucester, but this gathering was not a Parliament. Furthermore, the question of the legality of Edward IV's marriage because of a pre-contract could be decided only by a church court. Gloucester never submitted the pre-contract claim to such a court, possibly because he knew the story could not withstand a proper investigation.

No writer of the time believed the pre-contract story. The *Croyland Chronicle* called it "the colour [excuse] for this act of usurpation [taking over]." Neither is it likely that very many in the crowd listening to Buckingham believed it. Mancini wrote that those who accepted the story did so out of fear. They knew that Gloucester had sent for troops from the north. Mancini said that the nobles, consulting "their own safety" and seeing themselves "surrounded and in the hands of the dukes" decided their wisest course of action was to declare Gloucester king.

On the same day, far to the north at Pontefract Castle, Rivers, Grey, Haute, and Vaughan were beheaded. The writers of the time all agreed that the four men had committed no crime. John Rous, writing after Gloucester's death, said that these supporters of

At some point after he heard of his brother's death, Richard made it his sole object to seize the crown. Here, Buckingham, the lord mayor, and others offer Richard the crown, which he accepted with feigned reluctance.

Edward V were "unjustly and cruelly put to death, being lamented by everyone, and innocent of the deed for which they were charged." Earl Rivers's execution was illegal in another respect as well, since he, as a member of the high nobility, had a right to a trial before his fellow nobles.

A Reluctant King

On the following day, June 25, Buckingham led a delegation of nobles and citizens to Baynard's Castle, the home of Gloucester's mother, who apparently had forgiven him for Shaa's sermon. Once there, More wrote, Buckingham sent word to Gloucester that the assembly had a "great matter" to discuss. Gloucester sent word that he must know something more about their errand "as though he doubted and partly distrusted" the delegation. Buckingham used this message to try to show those he had brought with him that Gloucester had no idea why they were there.

At last, Gloucester came out onto a balcony overlooking the delegation. Buckingham, as spokesman, read the petition and pleaded with the duke to take the crown. Gloucester replied that because of "the love he bore unto King Edward [IV] and his children . . . that he could not find it in his heart in this point to incline [agree] to their desires." Buckingham renewed his plea, saying that the leading men of England were determined that the sons of Edward IV would not rule, and that if Gloucester did not accept the crown, they would have to find another noble who would.

Finally, More relates, Gloucester said:

> Since we perceive well that all the realm is so set, though we be very sorry that they will not suffer [allow] in any wise King Edward's line to govern them whom no man on earth can govern against their wills, and since we well also perceive that no man is there to whom the crown can by so just title appertain [belong] to as ourself . . . we be content and agree favourably to incline to your petition and request.

Those who heard this speech knew perfectly well that Gloucester and Buckingham had arranged the whole thing, but no one dared to speak out. More compared the scene to a theatrical performance and wrote, "In them [plays] poor men be lookers on, and they that wise be, will meddle no further."

Later that day, Gloucester, now known as King Richard III, rode to Westminster Hall and took his seat on the marble throne known as the King's Bench. He then went to Westminster Abbey to receive the scepter of Edward the Confessor, king of England from 1042 to 1066, as the monks chanted, probably within the hearing of Elizabeth Woodville, still in sanctuary. Then he rode to St. Paul's Cathedral to hear his title proclaimed to the public.

Richard wears the royal crown of the king of England.

Richard's Rewards

During the next few days, Richard rewarded those who had helped put him on the throne. Buckingham, Catesby, and Howard received additional land and titles. In a show of mercy, Richard released some of the former councilors who had been held prisoners since June 13. Lord Stanley, in fact, was named Lord Steward of the King's Household. Bishop Morton, however, was thought to be too dangerous. He was sent in Buckingham's custody to Brecknock Castle in Wales. It was a decision Richard would have cause to regret.

On July 3, Richard's army arrived from the north. The Londoners were somewhat relieved to see that the soldiers were poorly equipped and that their armor was rusty. Nevertheless, the presence of six thousand armed men ensured that there would be no trouble at Richard's coronation, scheduled for July 6. Richard reviewed the troops in person, riding among them and accepting their shouts of praise.

On July 4, Richard and his wife, Anne, daughter of the late Richard Neville, earl of Warwick, went by boat from Westminster to the Tower of London. That night, for the only time in history, two kings of England—Edward V and Richard III—slept in the Tower.

The coronation on July 6 was one of the most magnificent in the country's history. Most of the nobles of England were there, having come for the Parliament that had been scheduled for June 25. Many wore fine clothes that had been made in anticipation of Edward V's coronation. Others, perhaps Richard's followers who had not planned on attending a coronation, had kept tailors busy with rush orders. The keeper of the wardrobe, at one point, made a bookkeeping entry for clothes for "many divers persons, for to have in haste, by my Lord Buckingham's commandment, whose names were not remembered."

King Richard wore a blue doublet with a long gown of purple velvet trimmed with ermine. Anne wore purple robes that had been made from fifty-six yards of cloth. Mancini wrote that as Richard rode from the Tower to Westminster Abbey for the ceremony, he "greeted all onlookers, who stood along the streets, and himself received their acclamations." With him rode three dukes, nine earls, and twenty-two barons.

The Young Earl of Warwick

One of the most pathetic figures in English history is the princes' cousin Edward, earl of Warwick. Born in 1475, Edward was the son of George, duke of Clarence, the brother of Edward IV and Richard III.

Edward was three years old when his father was executed, but he was not allowed to inherit the title of duke of Clarence. He was earl of Warwick through his mother, however, since his grandfather Richard Neville had left no sons.

Brought by his uncle to London in 1483, after his two cousins had been taken into custody, Edward had been confined, not in the Tower, but in the household of Richard's wife, Anne.

After Richard was crowned, Edward was allowed to accompany him on his royal progress through the kingdom. In 1484, Richard's only son died, and Edward was declared Richard's heir.

After Richard's death, Henry VII had Edward taken from what had been a gentle confinement and placed in the Tower of London. He never left it alive.

In 1499, Perkin Warbeck, who had pretended to be Edward V's younger brother, Richard, was imprisoned by Henry in the Tower of London after trying to escape from a less formidable prison. Historians have suggested that Henry, suspecting Warbeck might try to escape, had him placed in the same cell with Edward, hoping to dispose of both at the same time. The plan worked. Warbeck tried to escape and Edward foolishly accompanied him. Both were caught and executed.

The execution of Edward horrified the people of London. The young earl had committed no crime. His mental incompetency also aroused people's pity. When he was led out between two armed guards to be executed, he did not seem to know where he was going or why.

Henry, however, had an urgent reason for wanting Edward dead. He had arranged for a marriage between his son Arthur and Princess Catherine of Aragon, daughter of King Ferdinand of Spain. Ferdinand was afraid to send Catherine to England, thinking that while Edward, earl of Warwick, lived, the Tudors' hold on the throne was insecure. Therefore, Henry had to be put out of the way.

The Royal Procession

As the procession entered Westminster Abbey, Lord Stanley carried the ceremonial mace. His wife, Margaret Beaufort, mother of the exiled Henry Tudor, was one of the women carrying the queen's train—the part of the robe trailing behind. Buckingham carried the king's train, and Howard—newly created duke of Norfolk—carried the crown. Buckingham apparently was upset that Norfolk had been given the more prestigious position because he later left the coronation banquet early, "feigning [pretending] himself sick."

Richard was a shrewd politician. He knew his seizure of the throne was unpopular with many of the nobility and with the citizens of London. Robert Fabyan, a London merchant of the time who kept a journal called *The New Chronicles of England and France*, wrote that people who had "loved and praised him still as

Because he had seized the throne in such an underhanded manner, Richard III used every opportunity to give his coronation legitimacy, including an elaborate procession.

Protector, now murmured and grudged against him." Richard decided to try to win the hearts of his people by embarking on a lavish tour of the country. Such a tour was called a "progress," because the monarch progressed from one city to another, impressing the people with royal splendor.

Richard left London on July 20. With him went five bishops and some of the leading nobles; whether Buckingham was present is not clear. Richard left behind a city that had accepted him as king, but not with any great joy. Although there was much uncertainty as to what kind of king Richard would make, the principal question on people's lips was this: Where are the princes? The question, first asked in whispers, out of fear, soon became a murmur and finally a roar that would end in rebellion.

5 *Rumors and Rebellion*

While their uncle went through the pomp and ceremony that made him Richard III, king of England, the deposed king and his brother were moved deeper into the Tower of London. They were seen on fewer and fewer occasions and finally vanished altogether. Even before Richard's coronation, the whispering began that he had murdered his nephews.

When Edward V was first housed in the Tower in May, it was in the royal apartments that had been built adjoining the south side of the White Tower. Later, on June 16, he was joined there by his brother, the duke of York.

Richard and Edward V huddle in their room in the Tower, isolated from familiar faces. They no doubt spent much of their time contemplating their fate.

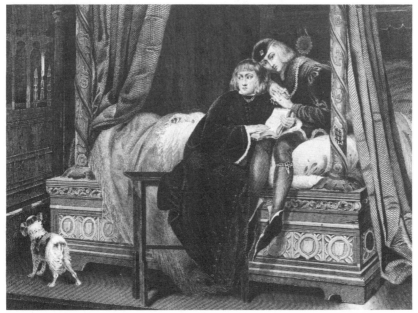

Richard occupied the royal apartments shortly before he was crowned, and the princes were moved, probably to the Garden Tower, so called because it stood beside the garden of the lieutenant of the Tower's residence. A compilation of historical writings entitled *The Great Chronicle of London* contains a report that during the time Edmund Shaa was mayor of London, from October 1482 to October 1483, "the children of King Edward were seen shooting [arrows] and playing in the garden of the Tower." The Garden Tower is now called the Bloody Tower, but it did not get that name until more than a hundred years later.

The Tower of London in the late fifteenth century was a semipublic place to which many people—visitors, merchants, soldiers—came each day. Richard had seen too many sudden shifts of fortune during the Wars of the Roses not to know that the princes were a danger to him. If they were freed, they could be the focus of rebellions as his enemies sought to replace him on the throne.

Therefore, the princes were moved once more, and the number of people who had access to them was strictly limited. As reported by Mancini:

> All the attendants who had waited upon the king were debarred access to him. He and his brother were withdrawn into the inner apartments of the Tower proper, and day by day began to be seen more rarely behind the bars and windows, till at length they ceased to appear altogether.

The White Tower

Mancini's "Tower proper" was almost certainly the White Tower, the central fortress of the Tower of London. The White Tower has three floors. The ground floor, in 1483, contained an armory where weapons and supplies were kept. The second was divided between the council chamber and the royal chapel. The third and uppermost floor contained rooms that had often been used to hold the most important prisoners. The princes were probably kept in a chamber on this floor.

On July 17 Richard appointed one of his most loyal followers, a northerner named Sir Robert Brackenbury, to be constable, or a chief officer, of the Tower. The next day, a royal order was issued authorizing payments to thirteen men for their services to "Edward, bastard, late called King Edward V." These were the servants Mancini described as "debarred," or kept away.

The White Tower, where the princes were moved after Richard's coronation. Even servants were not allowed to see them.

Other writers of the time described how security around the princes was increased. Robert Fabyan wrote in his chronicle that they were "under sure keeping. They never came abroad after." The *Croyland Chronicle* said that they "were in the Tower of London under special guard."

Although only twelve years old, Edward knew that the move into the White Tower and the replacement of the usual servants might be a sign of worse things to come for him and his brother. Mancini wrote that Dr. John Argentine,

> the last of his attendants whose services the king enjoyed, reported that the young king, like a victim prepared for sacrifice, sought remission [forgiveness] of his sins by daily confession and penance, because he believed that death was facing him.

Dr. Argentine may have been treating Edward for the diseased jaw discovered in an examination of the bones found under the Tower staircase in 1674. The pain he would have suffered might well have made him appear depressed.

The same view of Edward was repeated by Molinet, who wrote that, "The eldest [Edward] was simple and very melancholy, aware of the wickedness of his uncle." Molinet wrote that when Prince Richard asked Edward to dance, the older brother replied, "It would be better for us to learn to die, for I think we shall not long remain in the world."

Edward's apprehension was also reported by More, who doubtless interviewed persons who had been in a position to know what was happening. He wrote that the princes were

> both shut up, and all others removed from them, only one called Black Will or Will Slaughter except, set to serve them and see them sure. After which the Prince [Edward] never tied his points [shoelaces] nor aught wrought of himself, but with that young babe his brother lingered in thought and heaviness and wretchedness.

More wrote his *History of King Richard III* about 1515, but he could not have been merely copying Mancini, whom he never met, for the Italian author's manuscript was written as a report to the archbishop of Vienne in France and remained undiscovered until 1936.

Reports of Murder

It was Mancini who first reported rumors that the princes had been killed. He left England shortly before Richard's coronation and wrote:

> I have seen many men burst forth into tears and lamentations [expressions of sorrow] when mention was made of him [Prince Edward] after his removal from men's sight; and already there was a suspicion that he had been done away with. Whether, however, he has been done away with, and by what manner of death, so far I have not at all discovered.

With his nephews safely locked away, Richard left London on July 20 on his royal progress. About a week later, the first signs of rebellion appeared. The *Croyland Chronicle* reported that "in order to release them [the princes] from captivity, the people from the South and the West of the kingdom began to murmur greatly and to form assemblies and confederacies, many of which worked in secret, others openly with this aim."

At the center of the plot were the Woodvilles. Elizabeth and her daughters were still in sanctuary in Westminster Abbey, but Dorset had escaped about the time of Hastings's death, and Elizabeth's brother Lionel had been allowed to leave. Their goal was not, as the people in the south and west thought, to rescue Prince Edward, which would have been almost impossible, but to free Elizabeth's daughters and get them safely to France. In that way, the *Croyland Chronicle* said, "If any fatal mishap should befall the male children of the late King in the Tower, the kingdom might still, in consequence of the safety of the daughters, some day fall again into the hands of the rightful heirs."

Richard discovered the so-called Sanctuary Plot. Some historians believe the plotters tried to convince Buckingham to help them and that he reported their efforts to Richard. At any rate, on July 29 Richard sent word to his chancellor in London, Bishop Russell, and ordered that Westminster Abbey be surrounded, to foil any rescue attempt that might be made. Shortly, Westminster Abbey "assumed the appearance of a castle and fortress while men of the greatest austerity [grimness] were appointed by King Richard to act as the keepers thereof." The Sanctuary Plot failed, but the close call it seemed to represent may have convinced Richard that he would not be secure on the throne unless the princes were dead.

Buckingham's Rebellion

Another rebellion was soon to come. This one was much more serious because it involved the man closest to Richard—the duke of Buckingham. Historians disagree about why Buckingham turned against Richard. Some claim that he had been denied an inheritance, but the lands in question had already been granted to him by Richard. Others say that Buckingham wanted the throne for himself as a descendant of Edward III. This is unlikely, since the announced purpose of his rebellion was to place Henry Tudor on the throne.

It is of the greatest importance that what came to be called Buckingham's Rebellion was undertaken on Henry's behalf, not the young Edward's. The plan was that Henry, last hope of the house of Lancaster, would successfully invade England, aided by Buckingham, whereupon Henry would strengthen his claim by marrying Elizabeth, oldest daughter of Elizabeth Woodville and Edward IV.

What had happened to make Buckingham abandon Richard and support Henry Tudor? Why would Elizabeth Woodville abandon the claims of her sons to put a Lancastrian on the throne, even though one of her daughters would be queen? An obvious answer is that by this time, most of those involved believed that the young princes were dead.

Buckingham may or may not have accompanied Richard on his progress from London, but he was definitely with him in the city of Gloucester around August 1. There, Buckingham left the king and

Henry VII

went to his castle at Brecknock in Wales. More wrote that Buckingham, once at Brecknock, "so lightly turned from him [Richard] and so highly conspired against him that a man would marvel whereof the change grew."

Buckingham may have been told at Gloucester that Richard had ordered the princes murdered. Or Richard, who had no reason to doubt Buckingham's loyalty, may have written to him that the princes were dead. More wrote that Buckingham, however he received the news, told Bishop Morton, who had been in his custody since June, that "when he [Buckingham] was crediby informed of the death of those two infants, 'O Lord, how my veins panted, how my body trembled and my heart inwardly grudged.'"

Buckingham's Motives

Buckingham may have been moved more by self-interest than by conscience. The clever Morton may have persuaded his custodian that the murder of the princes would turn the entire country against Richard. Buckingham's wisest course of action, therefore, would be to abandon Richard, support Henry Tudor, and thus restore the house of Lancaster. Such an argument might well have appealed to Buckingham, whose grandfather had been killed fighting for the Lancastrian cause.

One of the principal figures in the plot was Margaret Beaufort, Henry Tudor's mother, now married to Lord Stanley. By coincidence

Margaret and Elizabeth Woodville had the same physician, a Dr. Lewis. By way of Dr. Lewis, Margaret, who had supposedly been informed of the princes' deaths by Buckingham, broke the news to their mother, who, according to Vergil,

> fell into a swoon and lay lifeless a good while; after coming to herself, she wept, she cried aloud, and with lamentable shrieks made all the house ring. She struck her breast, tore and cut her hair, and prayed also for her own death, calling by name her most dear children and condemning herself for a madwoman for that, being deceived by false promises, she had delivered her younger son out of sanctuary to be murdered by his enemy.

On September 24, Buckingham sent a letter to Henry in France pledging his support for an invasion. October 18 was selected as the date. The plan called for Henry's supporters in south and west England to form an army and march on London while, at the same time, Buckingham would advance with his troops from Wales and join Henry, who would land on the southwestern coast.

Nothing went as planned. Henry sailed from Brittany on October 3, but a violent storm forced his ships back to port. His supporters in Kent, southeast of London, began their revolt on October 10, a week too early. John Howard, duke of Norfolk, Richard's close ally, immediately moved south and blocked the rebels' crossing of the Thames River. Norfolk learned about Buckingham's change of sides from some captured rebel leaders and sent word to the king.

Quick Reaction

Richard acted quickly. He sent word to his supporters in Wales to "pounce upon all his [Buckingham's] property" if he moved from his castle. So it was that when Buckingham set out with an army on October 18, intending to cross the Severn River and join Henry, a neighbor of Buckingham's loyal to Richard moved in and captured his castle. Even the weather worked in Richard's favor. Ten straight days of heavy rain had caused such a rise in the Severn River that Buckingham could not cross. Unable to return to his castle and deserted by his troops, he took refuge with one of his tenants, who betrayed him to Richard's men. On November 2 he was executed in the marketplace at Salisbury.

On the same day, Henry's ships were finally able to reach England. He approached the harbor city of Plymouth. Armed men went to meet him in a small boat. Claiming to be Buckingham's soldiers, they assured him all was well. Henry was suspicious and later sent spies into the city. When he learned that Buckingham's planned rebellion had failed, he sailed back to France.

It seemed as if Richard had won. Buckingham was dead, and Henry Tudor had been forced to return to France. Actually, however, Richard's reign had received a wound that would prove to be fatal. The *Croyland Chronicle* said that just before Buckingham's Rebellion was to take place, "a rumour was spread that the sons of King Edward [IV] had died a violent death, but it was uncertain how." Followers of Buckingham and Margaret Beaufort spread this news across England.

Margaret Beaufort, mother of Henry VII, told Elizabeth Woodville that her sons had been murdered by Richard III.

Some historians believe that this claim was only a rumor intended to turn the public against Richard, and doubt that Buckingham and Margaret believed it to be true. This is very unlikely. Buckingham and Margaret very probably believed the princes to be dead. Otherwise, it would have been a simple matter for Richard to answer their accusations by producing his nephews. Indeed, that Richard, in the face of the rumors, failed to show the boys were still alive may have been the surest indication that they were not.

A Kingdom Mourns

The damage had been done. The entire country believed that Richard had ordered the princes murdered. Fabyan wrote in his historical chronicle, "It was common fame [knowledge] that King Richard had within the Tower put unto secret death the two sons of his brother Edward IV." Vergil wrote that "when the fame of this notable foul fact was dispersed through the realm, so great grief struck literally to the heart of all men that the same, subduing all fear, wept everywhere." Kings in other European countries believed it, too. King Louis XI of France, Commynes wrote, told his court that Richard was responsible for having "the two sons of his brother Edward put to death."

The fifteenth century was a rough, cruel time. England had been at war, either war with France or a civil war, for most of the last one hundred and fifty years. Slaughter on the battlefield, the killing of helpless prisoners, quiet murders in dark dungeons—all these were part of the times. Yet, the murder, or reported murder, of the princes shocked everyone. Why? The victims were children. Edward Hall, writing in the next century, explained:

> To murder a man is much odious, to kill a woman is in a manner unnatural, but to slay and destroy innocent babes and young infants the whole world abhorreth [despises], and the blood from the earth cries for vengeance to Almighty God. Alas, whom will he save when he slayeth the poor lambs committed to him in trust?

The remainder of Richard III's reign was short and filled with sorrow. On April 9, 1484, his son, Edward, died. Many people saw the death as Richard's punishment from God for the princes' murders. More wrote, "Many Englishmen declared that the imprecations [curses] of the agonised mother [Elizabeth Woodville] had been heard."

Richard's Nightmares

After the Battle of Bosworth, the story grew up that Richard III had been plagued by terrible dreams during the night before the battle. In his history of England, Polydore Vergil repeats the tale, attributing the dreams to a guilty conscience:

> [Richard] had that night a terrible dream; for he thought in his sleep that he saw horrible images as it were of evil spirits haunting evidently about him, as it were before his eyes, and that they would not let him rest. . . . But (I believe) it was no dream, but a conscience guilty of heinous [shocking] offences, a conscience (I say) so much the more grievous as th' offences were more great.

Vergil's story was picked up by later Tudor historians Edward Hall and Raphael Holinshed and at last was brought to the popular stage by William Shakespeare in his *Richard III*. In Shakespeare's version, two tents are shown onstage. In one sleeps Richard; in the other, Henry Tudor.

One after another, the ghosts of all the persons Richard is supposed to have killed—his brother, the duke of Clarence; Henry VI, Henry VI's son Edward, Rivers, Grey, Vaughan, and Hastings; the two princes; Queen Anne; and Buckingham (whose execution Richard had indeed ordered)—come onto the stage. Each ghost tells Richard to "think on me" during the upcoming battle and die. The two princes, for instance, say:

> Dream on thy cousins [relatives] smother'd in the Tower;
> Let us be lead within thy bosom, Richard,
> And weigh thee down to ruin, shame, and death!
> Thy nephews' souls bid thee despair and die!

When he awakens, Richard says, "Soft! I did but dream. O coward conscience, how dost thou afflict me!"

More personal sorrow lay ahead for Richard, as well as a scandal. By Christmas, it was apparent that Queen Anne was dying. It also appeared that a new queen might be on the horizon—Edward IV's eighteen-year-old daughter, named Elizabeth after her mother.

Sometime during the summer of 1484, the dowager queen had finally been convinced to emerge from Westminster Abbey. At Christmas, the *Croyland Chronicle* said, "the lady Elizabeth was, with her four younger sisters, sent by her mother to attend the Queen [Anne] at court." No one knows exactly what kind of attraction, if any, there was between Richard and his lovely niece. It may have been that a marriage with young Elizabeth would solve two political problems. First, he would have had a chance to father another son to inherit the throne after him. Second, if he married Elizabeth, she couldn't marry Henry Tudor.

A Chance for Power

It may have been, also, that Elizabeth and her mother were attracted by the idea of the marriage. Even though it is likely that the former

Elizabeth of York may have agreed to marry Richard III, her family's enemy, but Richard's advisers told him doing so would ruin him in the public's favor. Instead, Elizabeth married Henry VII.

queen believed Richard to be the murderer of the princes, she had always sought power. A chance to make her daughter queen and restore the fortunes of the Woodvilles would have been very tempting.

Anne died on March 16, 1485. The country, however, refused to condone even the idea of a marriage between the newly widowed king and his niece. Richard's closest advisers, Sir Richard Ratcliffe and the ever-present William Catesby, advised him that

> if he did not abandon his intended purpose and deny it by public declaration, all the people of the north, in whom he placed the greatest trust, would rise in rebellion and impute to him the death of the Queen, through whom he had first gained his present high position, in order that he might gratify his incestuous passion of his niece, something abominable before God.

Richard took their advice and at a large public gathering "showed his grief and displeasure and said it never came in his thought or mind to marry in such manner-wise."

With the prospect of her daughter's becoming queen by marrying Richard gone, Elizabeth Woodville agreed to support a plan to achieve the same goal by having the young woman marry Henry Tudor. Gradually, more and more nobles who either were supporters of the Woodvilles or enemies of Richard made their way to France and swore their loyalty to Henry.

Finally, on August 7, 1485, Henry and a small army landed on the southwest coast of Wales. Since the Tudors were a Welsh family, Henry could depend on the Welsh to rally to him. Richard managed to raise a large army—about ten thousand men. The army marched west to meet Henry. On August 21, it left the city of Leicester and camped that night near the small town of Market Bosworth. Henry's army, about half the size of Richard's, was about three miles away.

The Battle of Bosworth

On the next day, August 22, Richard III's reign—and his life—came to an end. As had happened so many times during the Wars of the Roses, the battle was decided by treachery. Sir William Stanley, Margaret Beaufort's brother-in-law, changed sides at the last minute, and one of Richard's most trusted allies, the duke of Northumberland, sat back and refused to enter the fighting.

Richard and His Niece

A scandal almost as explosive as the suspected murders of the princes in the Tower took place in 1485 when rumors spread that King Richard III intended to marry his niece Elizabeth, oldest daughter of Edward IV and Elizabeth Woodville. It was even whispered that Richard's wife, Anne, who had died in March 1485, had been poisoned by the king to get her out of the way.

Even if Richard had planned to marry Elizabeth Woodville, he was convinced by his closest advisers that the country would never stand for it and might rebel against him. Richard had to publicly declare that it had never been his intention to marry his niece.

Historians who defend Richard deny that he ever had such plans, but there is some evidence that the young Elizabeth not only longed for such a marriage but may have been Richard's mistress. Sir George Buck, writing in the seventeenth century, claimed to have seen a letter, saved by the Howard family as an heirloom, written by Elizabeth to John Howard, duke of Norfolk, one of Richard's most trusted men.

In the letter, Buck wrote, Elizabeth "prayed him [Norfolk], as before, to be a mediator for her in the cause of the marriage to the King who, as she wrote, was her only joy and maker in this world, and that she was his in heart and in thought, in body and in all."

While some later historians say Buck invented this letter, which has since been lost, there is no reason for him to have done so. In general, he was a defender of Richard III, and his great-grandfather was executed after fighting for Richard at Bosworth.

Others have suggested that the letter was a forgery, even though Buck believed it to be genuine. Yet, it is hard to imagine anyone with a reason to forge such a letter or the courage to do so in Tudor times, when Elizabeth's husband, son, and grandchildren occupied the throne.

Elizabeth, daughter of Edward IV.

As the battle raged, Richard decided to risk everything on one last, reckless charge. If he could only kill Henry Tudor, he might yet win. He fought furiously, but at last was overwhelmed and "alone was killed fighting manfully in the thickest press of his enemies."

Henry Tudor thus became King Henry VII. One of his first acts was to have Richard condemned by Parliament for treason. Since a king could not commit treason against himself, Henry dated his reign from August 21, the day before the Battle of Bosworth. The Act of Parliament accused Richard of "unnatural, mischievous and great perjuries [lies], treasons, homicides and murders in shedding of infants' blood."

The expression "infants' blood" was Henry's only reference to the princes. He wanted to be more specific—to blacken Richard's

During the Battle of Bosworth, Richard III (on white horse) makes one final charge at Henry VII's troops, only to be killed in battle.

In this dramatization, Henry VII is crowned on the field after the Battle of Bosworth.

reputation as much as possible. In all probability, he couldn't. Like everyone else, he thought Richard had caused the deaths of the princes, but he had no proof. He searched, one chronicle says, but could not find the bodies. The fate of Edward V and his brother was still a mystery. Only after another fifteen years had passed would more be learned about what had become of the princes in the Tower.

6 A Confession and Two Historians

After the death of Richard III at the Battle of Bosworth, Henry Tudor married Elizabeth of York—daughter of Edward IV and Elizabeth Woodville—and took the throne as Henry VII. How—or even if—the sons of Edward IV had met their deaths remained a mystery. It was not until the next century that information concerning the murders came to light, and there is disagreement about these materials, as well.

Although almost everyone thought the princes were dead by 1485, no one was certain, and some people put this uncertainty to their own use. Twice during his reign, Henry VII faced rebellions intended to place on the throne a person claiming to be Richard, duke of York, the younger prince.

Lambert Simnel (sitting at fireplace) claimed to be the missing Prince Richard. He ended up working in the royal kitchen of Henry VII.

Perkin Warbeck claimed to be an illegitimate son of Edward IV. His claim was more widely accepted than Lambert Simnel's.

The first such claimant was Lambert Simnel, son of a cook in Oxford. With his good looks and blond hair, he resembled members of the Plantagenet family. He was also highly intelligent and learned quickly when a priest named Richard Symonds coached him to play the part of the duke of York. Simnel won the support of Margaret, duchess of Burgundy, a sister of Edward IV and Richard III, who hated Henry VII. The boy was crowned "Edward VI" in Ireland and, with soldiers paid for by Margaret, invaded England in 1487. The invasion was crushed by Henry VII, and Symonds was thrown into the Tower. However Simnel—who was only about twelve years old—was pardoned by Henry and sent to work in the royal kitchen.

The other pretender was named Perkin Warbeck. He looked so much like a Plantagenet that some people thought that even if he were not the duke of York, he might be an illegitimate son of Edward IV. Many Yorkist nobles rallied to support him. The king of Scotland believed his story, arranged a noble marriage for him, and loaned him troops with which to invade England. The invasion in

1497, however, was a failure, and Warbeck was captured. Henry was not as lenient this time. Warbeck was hanged in the Tower.

It is clear from these impersonations that there was some doubt that the princes had been murdered in 1483. In fact, it was not until well after 1500 that two men, Polydore Vergil and Thomas More, described in some detail what they believed had befallen Edward V and his brother. A primary source of information for both writers was a confession of the crime by Sir James Tyrell.

Sir James Tyrell

Tyrell had been in the service of Richard III for at least ten years. He had fought for the Yorkists at Tewkesbury and was knighted after the battle. He served Richard as constable (chief officer) of Cardiff Castle in Wales, fought for him in Scotland in 1482, and was then created a knight banneret, the next step below a baron. By the time Richard left London after his coronation, Tyrell had been made Master of the Horse (supervising the care of the many horses needed for the journey) and Master of the King's Henchmen, or pages.

James Tyrell views the bodies of the murdered princes. Tyrell was said to have confessed that he was ordered to have the princes killed, although no copy of the confession has been found.

When the Battle of Bosworth was fought, Tyrell was abroad, as captain of Guisnes Castle outside the English city of Calais in France. He was removed from all his offices by Henry VII, but in 1486 swore allegiance to the new king and was pardoned, after which his offices were restored. He served Henry faithfully until 1501, when he gave refuge to Edmund de la Pole, earl of Suffolk, whose mother was a sister of Edward IV. Suffolk was plotting to overthrow Henry VII. When Henry found out that Tyrell had offered to help Suffolk, he had Tyrell arrested and jailed in the Tower. Found guilty of treason on May 2, 1502, Tyrell was beheaded on May 6. Before his execution, however, he confessed—according to More and others—that he had, on Richard's orders, overseen the murders of the princes in the Tower.

No copy of Tyrell's confession has survived, and some historians say it never existed. Yet, even as early as 1484, a contributor to the *Great Chronicle of London*, in discussing the ways in which the princes may have been killed, wrote, "but howsoever they were put to death, certain it was before that day [Easter 1484] they were departed this world, of which cruel deed Sir James Tyrell was reported to be the doer."

Polydore Vergil, commissioned by Henry VII to write an "official" history of England, likewise accused Tyrell. According to Vergil, Richard decided while on his progress to have his nephews killed. The Sanctuary Plot had convinced him that "he could never be out of hazard [danger]" so long as the princes lived. The king then sent word to Sir Robert Brackenbury, constable of the Tower, ordering him to kill the princes "by some means convenient." Brackenbury, horrified, put off carrying out the order.

A Sorrowful Journey

Vergil wrote that Richard, who was in York for the ceremony that would make his son Prince of Wales, commanded Tyrell to go to London to kill the princes. Tyrell, Vergil wrote,

> being forced to do the king's commandment, rode sorrowfully to London, and, to the worst example that hath been almost ever heard of, murdered those babes of issue royal. This end had Prince Edward and Richard his brother; but with what kind of death these sely [innocent] children were executed it is not certainly known.

Sir Robert Brackenbury

Sir Robert Brackenbury played a brief but highly important role in the story of the murders in the Tower. Brackenbury was constable of the Tower at the time the princes disappeared, and no one could have gained access to them without his permission.

Brackenbury was from Durham in far northern England and had entered Richard III's service years before, when Richard was serving Edward IV as governor of the north. He rose swiftly and soon became treasurer of Richard's household. As one of Richard's most trusted men, he well may have been present when Edward V was seized at Stony Stratford.

He was known as being a man of honor and high character. The *Chronicle of Calais*, written during Richard's reign, referred to him as "gentle Brackenbury."

On July 17, 1483, he was appointed constable of the Tower by Richard. The constable was the person who had charge of the day-to-day operation of the facility. The chief officer was the lieutenant of the Tower. Since many of the records of the Tower from Richard's reign have been lost, it is unclear who the lieutenant was, but in any event this official did not normally live in the Tower.

According to Sir Thomas More, Brackenbury refused Richard's order to murder the princes, but obeyed a second order, to surrender the keys of the Tower to Sir James Tyrell. Brackenbury continued in Richard's service and was killed along with him at the Battle of Bosworth.

Historian Paul Murray Kendall argues in his biography of Richard III that Brackenbury was too honorable a man to have handed the keys over to Tyrell and that even if he had, he would never have continued to serve Richard after learning of the act he had unwittingly had a part in. It is possible, however, that Brackenbury was a simple, straightforward man, completely and totally loyal to Richard; in the eyes of such a man, the king of England, Richard, could do no wrong.

Vergil makes no mention of Tyrell's confession. Since he was Henry's official historian, he would have known about the document if it had existed. He would have had access to state records and would have talked to people in position to know the facts. Perhaps the details of the murder were not in the confession, and Vergil may have thought it not important enough to mention.

It remained for Sir Thomas More to relate the specific details. It was his story on which Shakespeare's *Richard III* was based, and it is his version that found its way into most history books.

More had sources of information not available to Vergil. Part of his boyhood was spent in the household of Bishop Morton, one of the key figures of Richard's reign. Morton, who might well have known the true fate of the princes, may have told it to More, one of his prize students.

More also was a good friend of Joyeuce Lee, to whom he dedicated a book in 1505. Lee was a nun in a convent near London, and More often visited her there. Living in the same convent were several noblewomen, including Elizabeth, daughter of Sir Robert Brackenbury, who had been killed at Bosworth, and Mary Tyrell, who was either sister or cousin of Sir James. These women very likely talked among themselves of past events and could have included More in their conversations.

An Unfinished Story

More wrote his *History of King Richard III* first in Latin in about 1515 and a version in English in the late 1520s. He did not write it for publication, but for his own intellectual stimulation. He never even finished the book. There are blank spaces in the manuscript where he could not remember a name or a date and perhaps meant to add them later. The work was not published until 1543, long after More's death.

More's account agrees with Vergil's in stating that Richard sent word to Brackenbury to kill the princes. More wrote that the message was carried by one John Green, "whom he specially trusted." Brackenbury replied to Green that he would never put the princes to death "though he should die therefor."

Green returned to Richard, who was now at Warwick, with news of Brackenbury's refusal. Richard, in More's words, said, "Ah, whom shall a man trust? Those that I have brought up myself, those that I had thought would most surely serve me, even those fail me, and at my commandment will do nothing for me."

At this point, one of Richard's pages supposedly told him that there was a man in the next room—Tyrell—who would do anything for the king. More said that Tyrell had hoped for greater rewards once Richard became king, but was excluded by Ratcliffe and Catesby. Richard sent Tyrell to London with a letter for Bracken-bury, ordering the constable to surrender all the keys of the Tower to Tyrell for one night "to the end he might there accomplish the King's pleasure in such thing as he had given him commandment."

That night—possibly September 6, 1483—Tyrell used the keys given to him by Brackenbury and went to the princes' cell. He had decided, More wrote,

> that they should be murdered in their beds. To the execu-tion whereof he appointed Miles Forest, one of the four that kept them, a fellow fleshed in murder before time [an experienced killer]. To him he joined one John Dighton, his own horsekeeper, a big broad strong knave. Then all the others being removed from them, this Miles Forest and John Dighton about midnight (the innocent children lying in their beds) came into the chamber, and suddenly lapped them up among the bedclothes—so bewrapped them and entangled them, keeping down by force the featherbed and pillows hard unto their mouths, that within a while, smothered and stifled, their breath failing, they gave up to God their innocent souls into the joys of heaven, leaving to the tormentors their bodies dead in bed.

A Secret Burial

When the princes were dead, Forest and Dighton called for Tyrell, who apparently had stayed outside the cell, to inspect the bodies. Tyrell then "upon the sight of them, caused those murderers to bury them at the stair-foot, meetly deep in the ground under a heap of stones." This detail would seem to confirm the identity of the skeletons found under the Tower staircase almost two hundred years later.

More's account of Richard III's reign is full of errors, however, and some of the most serious concern the deaths of the princes. For in-stance, he makes it sound as if Richard's page had to tell the king who Sir James Tyrell was. Tyrell, however, had been one of Richard's closest followers for years and surely was well known to the king.

More also wrote that Tyrell was sent from Warwick. Actually, records prove, he was dispatched by Richard from the city of York on September 2. The official reason for his errand was to fetch robes for the ceremony at which Richard's son would be created Prince of Wales. By leaving York on September 2, Tyrell would have had time to reach London by September 6.

An even greater error was More's account of what happened to the princes' bodies. He wrote that when Tyrell returned to Richard and told the king that his orders had been carried out, Richard was disturbed that the princes had been buried in "so vile a corner." Richard, indeed, seemed to take great pains to ensure that even his enemies received a fitting burial. He had the body of Henry VI moved to a place of honor at Windsor Castle and caused the body of Hastings to be buried next to that of Edward IV, Hastings's greatest friend. Thus, it was entirely in character that Richard, in More's story, had "a priest of Sir Robert Brackenbury" dig up the princes' bodies and rebury them "in such a place as, by the occasion of his [the priest's] death—for he alone knew it—could never come to light."

More wrote that even Tyrell and Dighton, when they were being questioned in the Tower in 1502, believed that the princes had

Two men prepare to suffocate the little princes with a featherbed. Some historians believe Miles Forest and John Dighton committed the crime.

been reburied, "but whither the bodies were removed they could nothing tell." More, however, was relying on people's recollection of events that had occurred thirty years before. In any event, if the skeletons found in 1674 *are* those of the princes, no reburial ever took place. Perhaps those who had spoken of Richard's order were not aware that it had not been carried out. It is unlikely that anyone would have checked.

The Revisionists

In the centuries since More's and Vergil's books were published, many historians, sometimes called revisionists because they have sought to revise the accepted view that Richard III had his nephews killed, have claimed Richard was innocent or at least have called into serious doubt whether he was guilty. To do so, they have tried to show that Vergil and More—especially More, who went into such great detail—were mistaken, misinformed, or deliberately wrote something they knew to be false.

The revisionists charged both More and Vergil with being "Tudor" historians—in other words, with wanting to please Henry VII by blackening Richard's reputation as much as possible. In Vergil's case, this might be true to some degree. The Italian was employed by Henry to write an official history. Those he talked to knew Henry had given his permission. In addition, Vergil had access to official and private papers. And yet, Vergil did not simply write what Henry wanted him to write. At several points in his history, he was critical of Henry, and he made Henry furious by writing that King Arthur had never existed. Henry claimed to be a descendant of Arthur and had named his first son after the legendary British hero.

It is much less likely that More's writing was in any way influenced by the thought of pleasing a king. First, More's long career showed an independence of spirit. In 1504 he opposed Henry VII in Parliament, greatly provoking the monarch. Later, More rose to become chancellor to Henry VIII, but he resigned from this high position as a matter of conscience and was, like the princes, imprisoned in the Tower of London. More could have secured his own release at any time by adopting a position that "pleased the king." He did not do this, however, and ultimately was executed.

The second reason for rejecting the idea that More wrote to please Henry is that unlike Vergil, More was not writing an official

Although some historians claim that Thomas More (pictured) wrote a history of the princes that would please Henry VII, he was probably far too independent to do this. Because of his independent thinking, he spent his last years just as the princes had—imprisoned in the Tower of London.

history. Since he was writing only for his own amusement and there is no evidence he even meant to have his book published, why would he alter the facts?

The revisionists also say that because of the numerous errors in More's story, none of it can be accepted as true. There are, in fact, many errors, but it should be remembered that unlike Vergil, More did not have access to official papers. Instead, More had to rely on conversations with people who were recalling long-ago events, and the blank spaces in his manuscript reveal that he was not sure enough of some information to write it down.

A Careful Scholar

If the revisionists are to be believed, More was a careless researcher and writer. The fact is that he was trained as a lawyer and

Sir Thomas More

Of all historians who have written about King Richard III and the murder of his nephews, the most influential has been Sir Thomas More. His story of Richard's reign, with its dramatic speeches and specific details, became the basis for most later works, including Shakespeare's *Richard III*.

Some revisionist historians who seek to defend Richard's reputation have claimed that More wrote his *History of King Richard III*, with its story of how Richard ordered the deaths of the princes, to please King Henry VII. It is difficult, however, given the well-documented story of More's career, to accept this line of thinking.

More was never one to let his own safety stand in the way of saying and writing what he thought was the truth. In the early days of his public service, as a member of Parliament, he once opposed Henry VII with unusual vigor. Henry, unable under the law to imprison any member of Parliament, was so angry that he had More's father, the judge, thrown in prison instead.

In fact, it was More's strength of character that brought about his death in 1535 under the next Tudor monarch, King Henry VIII. More was a dedicated defender of the Roman Catholic Church against Protestants such as Martin Luther. In 1520 he helped Henry VIII write a reply to Luther that earned Henry the title "Defender of the Faith." In 1532, however, when Henry threatened to break with the Catholic Church if the pope would not grant him a divorce, More resigned as Henry's chancellor, or chief minister.

Later, when Henry declared himself head of the Church of England, More refused to take an oath of loyalty. He was imprisoned in the Tower of London in April 1534, and beheaded on July 6, 1535. Before he died, he said he was "the king's good servant, but God's first." In 1935, he was made a saint by the Roman Catholic Church.

Thomas More's unwillingness to compromise his religious principles led to his beheading in 1535.

was considered to have one of the finest legal minds of his time. He was an expert at digging for evidence, then sifting through it to find the truth. In introducing his story of the deaths of the princes, More made it clear that he was not merely passing along gossip: "I shall rehearse you the dolorous [sad] end of those babes, not after every way that I have heard, but after that way that I have so heard by such men and by such means as methinks it were hard but [likely that] it should be true." And, when he had finished his tale, he wrote that his information had been "learned of them that much knew and little cause had to lie."

It is even possible that one of More's sources was Dighton, whom, he wrote, "yet walks alive, in good possibility to be hanged ere he die." From this, it seems clear that More knew that Dighton was still alive and possibly had talked with him.

One writer, Audrey Williamson, suggested that More never meant to write a history at all—that he made Richard III a villain of "horror-comic proportions, as a moral example, not a human portrait." No evidence exists to support this claim. Besides, if More was writing only for himself, for whom was the "moral example" intended?

More's story relies, in part, on Tyrell's confession. Some revisionists suggest that this confession was never made. If it had been, they argue, why was it not mentioned by Vergil, and why, if Henry VII at last had proof of Richard's guilt, did he not publish it?

First, Henry VII had a reputation as an extremely secretive person, one who, as historian Francis Bacon later wrote, was used to "showing things by pieces and by dark lights" rather than being honest and straightforward. It was Henry's habit to reveal as little as possible, and he had no wish to remind people about the house of York. Second, at the time of Tyrell's confession, Henry had recently executed the earl of Warwick, the mentally retarded son of Edward IV's brother, on a flimsy charge. He did not want any publicity about the deaths of the princes to remind people of his own guilty act. Third, Tyrell had prospered in Henry's service, and perhaps Henry feared that if the confession were made public, people would think that Tyrell had murdered the princes for Henry's sake, not for Richard's. Fourth, Tyrell's confession would be of use to Henry only if it could be proved, and the only possible proof would consist of the bodies. But Tyrell's confession was worthless to Henry because it stated that the bodies had been moved.

Some historians question why Henry VII, after hearing More's accusations of Tyrell as the killer of the princes, did not publicize the fact.

A Touchy Question

The deaths of the princes was still a very sensitive political issue in 1502. It is possible for that reason that Vergil, although naming Tyrell as the person who supervised the murders, gave no details. More found out about the confession years later and even then did not name his sources. Indeed, More may have decided not to write his book for publication in the first place because the issue remained so sensitive.

Other revisionists say Henry invented Tyrell's confession after Tyrell's execution. If this is true, it is hard to see why Henry did not publish it. Why would the king bother to fabricate a confession and then keep it a secret?

And finally, some historians question why Tyrell, who knew he was about to die, would take the trouble to confess to a crime almost twenty years in the past. It was possibly the death sentence itself that led Tyrell to confess to the murders of the princes. The vast majority of people in the Middle Ages were very religious, and Tyrell may have wanted to clear his pathway to heaven by purging his conscience of his great crime.

Tyrell also may have confessed in exchange for a pardon for his son Thomas. Thomas Tyrell, who had been arrested along with his father, was originally condemned to die, but Henry pardoned him and three years later restored to him the family estates.

Tyrell's confession, whether fiction or fact, and the writings of Vergil and More formed the foundation for the tradition that Richard III was responsible for the murder of the princes in the Tower. More's version, in particular, was accepted by later Tudor historians and by Shakespeare, who made the story one of the most popular and widely believed in all English history.

7 *Who Killed the Princes?*

The belief that James Tyrell oversaw the murder of the princes on Richard III's orders went unchallenged for more than one hundred years. Ever since the early 1600s, however, a steady stream of writers and historians have attempted to prove Richard innocent. Societies have even been organized in both Great Britain and the United States to defend his reputation.

Richard's defenders present various reasons for believing that the traditional story of the princes' deaths is false. They claim, for instance, that Richard would never have entrusted a letter ordering the murders to John Green. They say that Brackenbury, from all accounts an honorable man, would never have turned over his keys to Tyrell. They say that Elizabeth Woodville would never have considered permitting a marriage between one of her daughters and the man who murdered her young sons.

The revisionists, however, have always faced a major difficulty: if Richard did not kill the princes, who did? Those who set up reasonable arguments that Richard was not responsible are then at a loss to come up with a plausible culprit. These accounts of the crime, wrote Elizabeth Jenkins in *The Princes in the Tower*, "describe, often with admirable lucidity [clearness], the course of events leading up to the coronation of Richard III, but when they try to provide an alternative solution to the enigma [mystery] of the Princes' disappearance, they spin off into space." And A. R. Myers, a defender of Richard, wrote that "for alternate explanations no evidence (as distinct from speculation) has ever been offered."

A Vote for Henry VII

Sir Clements Markham, a historian of the Victorian era, wrote that the murderer was none other than Henry VII—that the princes were still prisoners in the Tower after Bosworth and that Henry had them killed as possible threats to his rule. He based his claim on the theory that Bishop Morton had invented the story about Tyrell and passed it on to an unsuspecting More. The problem with Markham's theory, as Charles Ross points out, is that "it is unsupported by any shred of direct evidence." And Myers suggests that if Henry were clever enough to have kept it secret that the princes lived for at least two years after 1483, he would have been able to invent a more believable story than Tyrell's confession and would have published it widely.

Audrey Williamson speculates that Dr. Argentine, mentioned by Mancini as having treated Edward V, might instead have killed him as "an agent of Henry Tudor" who used "means of his own to hasten the death of at least the elder prince." Once again, there is no evidence whatsoever to back this theory. In fact, Dr. Argentine has been found to have been a thoroughly respectable physician.

Richard III

John Howard, duke of Norfolk, has also come under suspicion as the murderer. Historian S. T. Bindoff argues that Norfolk was constable of the Tower early in 1483 and wanted to murder the princes, especially young Richard, who was duke of Norfolk in addition to duke of York, to get the Norfolk title for himself. Bindoff bases the theory on an entry from a Howard family record that shows an expense in the Tower for two sacks of lime, which might have been used to dissolve the bodies of the princes. But why would Norfolk resort to murder to remove the princes when young Richard had already been declared illegitimate and Norfolk had been granted his title? It also is doubtful that Howard was still constable of the Tower at the time the princes were imprisoned.

Buck's Theory

One of Richard's earliest defenders was Sir George Buck, whose book *The History of King Richard III* was written in 1619. Buck was a great-grandson of a member of Richard's personal staff who was executed after the Battle of Bosworth. He was careful in his research and was the first to try to clear Richard's name by dismissing More's story as being too full of errors.

One historian implicates John Howard, duke of Norfolk, as the killer of the little princes. Howard died supporting Richard at the Battle of Bosworth.

When it came to finding another suspect in the murders, however, Buck was less convincing. He claimed to have seen "an old manuscript book" showing that "Dr [Bishop] Morton and a certain Countess, contriving the death of Edward V and other, resolved it by poison." This statement ignores two important facts: first, the countess, by whom Buck meant Margaret Beaufort, would not have had any way to get into the Tower, and second, Morton was Buckingham's prisoner at the time More says the duke learned of the princes' deaths.

Buckingham, in fact, is a much more serious suspect than Henry, Norfolk, Argentine, Margaret Beaufort, or Morton. He is the only person other than Richard who was mentioned at the time of the princes' disappearance as having caused their deaths. Philippe de Commynes wrote that Buckingham "had put the two children to death, for Richard himself a few days afterwards ordered his execution." And another Frenchman, Jean Molinet, wrote that "on the day that Edward's sons were assassinated, there came to the Tower of London the Duke of Buckingham, who was believed, mistakenly, to have murdered the children in order to forward his pretensions to the crown."

In this century, Paul Murray Kendall has suggested Buckingham as a suspect but stops short of accusing him of the murders. Kendall points out that Buckingham had both motive and opportunity to kill the princes. His motive may have been to take the throne for himself, since he was a descendant of Edward III. If he did away with the princes and then led a successful rebellion against Richard, he might have become king. Kendall also argues that Buckingham, who was constable of England, would have had access to the Tower and to the princes and might have remained in London to carry out the murders after Richard left on his progress.

However, constable of England and constable of the Tower are two different positions. Richard's faithful friend Brackenbury, who *was* constable of the Tower, would have demanded a document signed and sealed by Richard himself before allowing Buckingham (and, presumably, one or more hired killers) anywhere near the princes.

Buckingham a Tool?

Kendall theorizes also that Buckingham might have murdered the princes on Richard's orders. In that case, however, why would Buckingham turn against Richard? And why, after the rebellion had been crushed and Buckingham executed, did Richard fail to add the children's murders to the list of the duke's crimes? With Buckingham executed, Richard could have claimed that any written order from him—without which Buckingham could never have gained access to the princes—was a forgery.

Other writers suggest that the princes were not murdered in the Tower at all—that they were sent elsewhere and lived well into the reign of Henry VII. Eighteenth-century historian Horace Walpole, in his *Historic Doubts Concerning the Life and Reign of King Richard III*, pointed to a list of clothing in the royal accounts, part of which were garments made for Richard's coronation. One of the items was for a robe for "the Lord Edward, son of the late King, Edward IV." In Walpole's interpretation Richard, far from having his nephew killed, meant for him to attend the coronation, and Edward may have actually done so.

But Richard had gone to considerable trouble to convince the people that his nephews were illegitimate. Why would he then remind them of the existence of Edward V by having the boy appear in public? In addition, modern scholars have decided that the wardrobe list referred to by Walpole was not drawn up until 1484

Prince Edward V

and contained clothing originally made for Edward V's coronation—the one that never took place.

Markham claimed that Richard had the princes secretly moved to a castle at Sheriff Hutton in Yorkshire. He based his theory on two old documents. One refers to the earl of Lincoln—a nephew of Richard's to whom he gave the castle—having breakfast with "the children." The other calls for the delivery of clothes to "Lord Bastard." The word "children," however, could have meant many others, including the younger daughters of Edward IV. And the "Lord Bastard" might well have been Richard's own illegitimate son, John of Gloucester.

Another Version

According to Audrey Williamson, the princes, instead of being killed by Tyrell, might have been taken to his castle, Gripping Hall. The main difficulty with the theories that the princes were taken from London to live elsewhere is that the many people who must have known about it would have left many more traces in documents, and at least some of those documents would probably have been discovered by now.

Kendall and others have tried to show that the skeletons found in the Tower in 1674 might not have been those of the princes. Kendall's medical experts, indeed, have shown that the bones *might* not be those of Edward V and Richard, but no one has come close to proving that they *are* not. Those who say the bones might be from earlier times, even as far back as the Roman occupation of Britain from 54 B.C. to A.D. 400, present no proof. This theory must be discarded, in any event, because the bones were found with velvet, which was not invented until the 1400s.

A Queen's Fate

With her enemy Richard III dead and her daughter Elizabeth queen of England, it must have seemed to Elizabeth Woodville that her troubles were at last at an end. However, more misfortune would come to this woman who had played such a pivotal role in the history of England.

In February 1487, Henry VII met with his council to discuss the threat posed by Lambert Simnel, who had once claimed to be Elizabeth's son Richard, the duke of York. Indeed, Sir Francis Bacon, writing in the next century, suggested that the pretender may have been coached by Elizabeth, among others, to play the part of Richard. Now, however, Simnel said he was Edward, earl of Warwick, son of Richard III's brother the duke of Clarence. Even though Edward was a prisoner in the Tower, Henry was afraid Simnel might become the center of a serious rebellion.

Part of the discussion of the council had to do with Elizabeth Woodville. She was stripped of all her lands and possessions on the charge that four years earlier, she had surrendered her daughters to Richard III from the sanctuary of Westminster Abbey. On February 20, Parliament declared all Elizabeth's estates forfeited and granted her the modest (for a former queen) income of 400 marks a year. The real reason for Henry's action against his mother-in-law was probably greed, since the income from all of Elizabeth's former property was ordered paid to her daughter, Henry's wife.

Deprived of most of her income, Elizabeth Woodville, whose beauty and greed had almost torn England apart, retired to a nunnery where she lived quietly, only occasionally visiting the royal court, until her death in 1492. She was buried at Windsor Castle alongside her husband, Edward IV.

Thomas B. Costain, in his book *The Last Plantagenets*, claims that the scientists who first examined the bones were wrong in estimating the ages at the time of death. He argues that since people were shorter on average in the fifteenth century than today, ages arrived at by comparing the height of the skeletons against present-day averages are likely to be incorrect. Costain overlooks one undisputed historical fact, however: the Plantagenet family was

Richard on Trial

Almost five hundred years after his death, King Richard III was placed on trial, accused of the murders of his nephews in the Tower of London. The "trial" was conducted in 1984 by a British television network.

The trial featured an actual judge. Prominent attorneys argued for the prosecution and for the defense. Actors portraying men and women prominent in the case gave their testimony, dressed as they would have been in 1483.

Other witnesses included historians, who commented on the reliability of letters and chronicles, and medical experts, who testified on the skeletons that had been found in the Tower in 1674. At the end of the trial, Richard III was found "not guilty" by a jury. However, as Alison Weir observed in her book *The Princes in the Tower:*

"Historians . . . are not, and should not be, bound by the same rules as juries. . . . A jury must be satisfied beyond a reasonable doubt that a person is guilty of a crime; a historian constructs his theory on a balance of probabilities. In this case [Richard's], there are facts and the testimony of witnesses as well as probabilities, and the historian is perhaps therefore in a better position than a modern jury to arrive at the truth."

known for its tall men. The princes' father, Edward IV, at six foot, six inches, was tall even by today's standards.

Many of the theories suggesting that someone other than Richard III murdered his nephews or that the princes escaped are pure guesswork. Charles Ross, in his biography of the king entitled *Richard III*, has noted that most of the authors who defend Richard are not respected historians, but include a law professor, a school headmaster, and "a number of historical novelists and writers of detective stories." He adds, "Far too much of the pro-Ricardian stance rests on hypothesis and speculation, on a series of unconnected 'ifs' and 'buts,' on the 'may have been,' or even worse . . . the 'must have been.'"

The revisionists have used similar arguments in attempting to show that Richard did not order his nephews killed. Horace Walpole, in *Historic Doubts*, claimed that Richard was not suspected of the crime during his lifetime and that the Tudor historians Vergil and More had invented their stories to please Henry VII. This has been a common theme of pro-Richard writers ever since. The only trouble with the theory is that both Vergil and More—especially More—exhibited independence of thought during their careers. Furthermore, More's book was not written for publication.

Mancini's Revelation

The notion that there was no suspicion of Richard at the time of the princes' disappearance was overturned in 1936 with the discovery of Dominic Mancini's manuscript—an account by an eyewitness, a foreigner who had no reason to be for or against Richard. Even this find, however, did not stop some of the revisionists, who claimed that Mancini, not understanding English, probably got many of his facts wrong. According to Charles Ross, these claims "rest on mere biased [prejudiced] speculation and do not deserve serious consideration."

Other writers have pointed to More's mistakes and have said that nothing he wrote can be relied on to be true. Still others have tried to dismiss More's book as fiction. None of them, however, has been able to prove that this well-qualified author's account of the murders is false.

The writers who do not accept More's version also dismiss as unreliable the *Croyland Chronicle*, written during Richard's reign. This work states specifically that Richard murdered his nephews and that most people at the time suspected him. Sir Clements Markham, writing in 1891, rejected the chronicle as being the work of "credulous [naive or trusting] old Croyland monks." Later historians, however, have shown that the writer of the portion of the *Croyland Chronicle* dealing with Richard III's reign was probably Bishop John Russell, a member of the royal council, who was in a position to know all that was happening.

Richard III

The Tudors' Brutality

While the enduring image of Richard III is that of a thoroughly evil monster, his immediate successors have had better press.

Richard's bad reputation has come about mostly because of the belief that he had his nephews, the princes in the Tower, murdered. Similar crimes, however, can be laid at the feet of both Henry VII and Henry VIII.

After Henry VII's victory at Bosworth, most people assumed that Edward, earl of Warwick, the son of Richard III's late brother the duke of Clarence, would be treated with the same kindness Richard had shown to his unfortunate young kinsman.

To Henry, however, the gentle, slow-witted Edward was a potential rival. The Tudor victory at Bosworth would have counted less if Yorkist partisans had decided to rally around the young earl of Warwick. Therefore Henry had the youth imprisoned in the Tower of London, where he remained for fourteen years.

In 1499, under the influence of the pretender Perkin Warbeck, Edward tried to escape from the Tower. The plan failed, however, and Henry had both young men put to death. Warbeck was charged with treason, which was a serious offense, but the execution of Edward, a childlike innocent who had committed no crime, brought Henry intense criticism.

Henry VIII went even further to eradicate the house of York, turning his attention to Margaret, only remaining child of the duke of Clarence, and Katherine, Edward IV's youngest daughter. These noble ladies had married Sir Richard Pole and Sir William Courtenay, respectively.

In 1539, suspecting a plot, Henry VIII imprisoned the sons of Margaret and Katherine—Henry Pole and Henry Courtenay—along with these gentlemen's twelve-year-old sons. Both Pole and Courtenay were executed.

Two years later, Henry had Margaret, then an old woman, executed. Henry Pole, Margaret's grandson, died in the Tower, and some claimed he was starved to death on Henry VIII's orders. Edward Courtenay, however, was finally released in 1553 by Henry VIII's daughter Queen Mary I.

If no other suspects can be proven guilty of the murder of the princes, can one assume Richard is guilty? Not at all. Major difficulties remain in Thomas More's story. It still seems strange to many historians that Henry VII did not publish Tyrell's confession, despite the reasons he may have had for not doing so. Most troublesome of all is the question of why, if Tyrell confessed, did Henry not search for the bodies in the place where Tyrell said they had been buried? It is known that Henry had "all places opened and digged" in the Tower trying to locate the princes' bodies. Even if Tyrell was convinced the bodies had been moved, it is unlike the careful, methodical Henry not to have dug one last time in the place the confessed murderer had identified as the original place of burial.

The Most Likely Suspect

Yet, of all the suspects in the deaths of the princes in the Tower, the evidence points most strongly to their uncle, King Richard III. Alison Weir sums up:

> In conclusion, then, we may say that the evidence overwhelmingly suggests that the Princes were murdered by Richard III in 1483, that this was what Richard's contemporaries and later generations believed had happened, and that Sir Thomas More's account is very near to the truth. It would be comforting to present the revisionist theory as fact, but there is just not the evidence to substantiate [confirm] it.

Detectives, when investigating a murder, ask themselves two questions: did the suspect have a motive for murder, and did the suspect have an opportunity? Richard III had both. In addition to having complete control of the princes, Richard needed their deaths to ensure his hold on the throne, just as earlier monarchs who had seized their crowns by force had done away with those whose places they took. As Richard's biographer Kendall observes, "The dismissing of a king from his throne is but the first step in dismissing him from the world. A deposed monarch has nowhere to fall but into the grave."

Yet, there is no direct evidence, other than Tyrell's supposed confession in 1502 and the discovery of the skeletons in 1674, to support More's story. Instead, the strongest evidence against Richard was provided by Richard himself. During and after the rebellion of Buckingham, rumors spread throughout England that Richard had ordered the murder of the princes. To a great extent, it was people's revulsion at the rumored murders that caused them to desert Richard and turn to Henry Tudor.

If, as some historians claim, Richard did not kill his nephews but kept them prisoners in the Tower, why didn't he stop the rumors by producing the boys? Certainly, they were a danger to him while they were alive, but the widespread belief that they had been murdered was far worse for Richard. As Myers points out, "The most powerful indictment of Richard is the plain and massive fact that the princes disappeared from view after he assumed the throne and were never again reported to have been seen alive."

The mysterious deaths of the little princes in the Tower have been debated for more than five hundred years. No final solution has been found. None is in sight. It may be that history will never know exactly what happened to King Edward V and his younger brother after they entered the Tower of London.

And yet, who knows what documents may still lie, undiscovered, in some shadowy corner of some obscure vault? After all, Mancini's book, one of the most important in the case, did not come to light until 1936. And who knows what, after another five hundred years have passed, may be found behind some wall or underneath some floor in the Tower of London? That forbidding fortress on the banks of the Thames may yet yield up one of her most mysterious secrets.

Appendix A

The Woodvilles

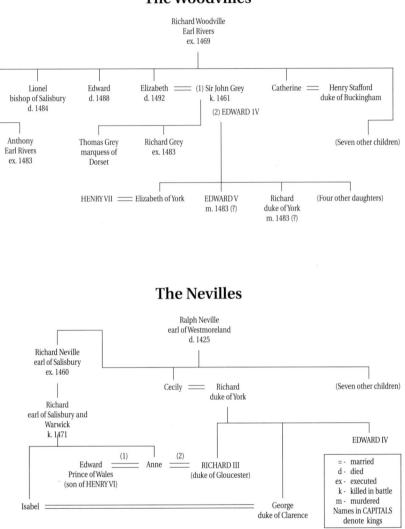

The Nevilles

Appendix B

Lancaster, York, and Tudor

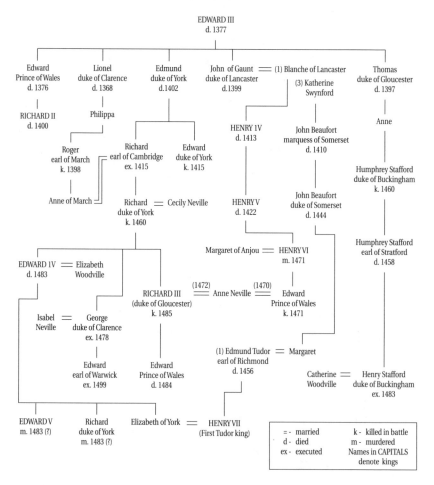

EDWARD III
d. 1377

Edward
Prince of Wales
d. 1376

RICHARD II
d. 1400

Lionel
duke of Clarence
d. 1368

Philippa

Edmund
duke of York
d.1402

John of Gaunt = (1) Blanche of Lancaster
duke of Lancaster
d.1399   (3) Katherine
              Swynford

Thomas
duke of Gloucester
d. 1397

Anne

HENRY IV
d. 1413

John Beaufort
marquess of Somerset
d. 1410

Roger
earl of March
k. 1398

Richard
earl of Cambridge
ex. 1415

Edward
duke of York
k. 1415

Humphrey Stafford
duke of Buckingham
k. 1460

Anne of March

Richard = Cecily Neville
duke of York
k. 1460

HENRY V
d. 1422

John Beaufort
duke of Somerset
d. 1444

EDWARD IV = Elizabeth
d. 1483   Woodville

Margaret of Anjou = HENRY VI
                    m. 1471

Humphrey Stafford
earl of Stratford
d. 1458

RICHARD III
(duke of Gloucester)
k. 1485

(1472)   (1470)
= Anne Neville =   Edward
                   Prince of Wales
                   k. 1471

Isabel = George
Neville   duke of Clarence
          ex. 1478

Edward
earl of Warwick
ex. 1499

Edward
Prince of Wales
d. 1484

(1) Edmund Tudor = Margaret
earl of Richmond
d. 1456

Catherine = Henry Stafford
Woodville   duke of Buckingham
            ex. 1483

EDWARD V
m. 1483 (?)

Richard
duke of York
m. 1483 (?)

Elizabeth of York = HENRY VII
                    (First Tudor king)

= - married	k - killed in battle
d - died	m - murdered
ex - executed	Names in CAPITALS denote kings

102

Chronology

1464
King Edward IV marries Elizabeth Woodville in secret ceremony (May 1)

1470
Future King Edward V is born in Westminster Abbey (November 2)

1471
Edward IV defeats Lancastrians at Battles of Barnet and Tewkesbury; King Henry VI murdered in Tower of London

1473
Richard, younger son of Edward IV, born (August 17)

1483
April 9—Edward IV dies

April 11 (?)—Lord Hastings writes to Richard, duke of Gloucester, advising him of Edward IV's death

April 14—Edward V's uncle, Earl Rivers, receives letter at Ludlow Castle telling him to bring the young king to London as soon as possible

April 24—Rivers and Edward V leave Ludlow

April 30—Gloucester and duke of Buckingham arrest Rivers at Northampton, take control of Edward V at Stony Stratford

May 1—Edward V's mother, Elizabeth Woodville, and her relatives, including Prince Richard, take refuge in Westminster Abbey

May 4—Edward V, accompanied by Gloucester and Buckingham, rides into London and is housed at the palace of the bishop of London

May 10—Royal council formally grants Gloucester title of protector

May 10–19—Edward V is moved to the Tower of London

June 10—Gloucester writes city of York to send armed troops

June 13—Gloucester has Hastings executed; Morton and others are arrested

June 16—Prince Richard is released from sanctuary by his mother; joins Edward V in the Tower

June 17—Gloucester postpones coronation of Edward V

June 22—Ralph Shaa preaches sermon in London claiming King Edward IV was illegitimate

June 24—Buckingham speaks to large assembly, claiming the princes were illegitimate and that Gloucester should be made king

June 25—Buckingham presents petition to Gloucester, who agrees to take throne; Gloucester receives royal scepter and is proclaimed King Richard III at St. Paul's Cathedral

July 6—Coronation of King Richard III

July 17—Richard III's follower, Sir Robert Brackenbury, made constable of the Tower; most of the princes' attendants are dismissed

July 20—Richard III leaves London on royal progress

July 29—Richard III writes to Bishop Russell to increase guard at Westminster Abbey in response to Sanctuary Plot

September 2—Sir James Tyrell sent by Richard III from York to London

September 6 (?)—Tyrell oversees murder of princes by Miles Forest and John Dighton

September 24—Buckingham writes to Henry Tudor, pledging his support in a rebellion against Richard III

October 3—Henry Tudor sails from Brittany but is forced back by storms

October 10—Rebellion begins prematurely in Kent, is put down by duke of Norfolk

October 18—Buckingham's army sets out but is unable to cross Severn River because of floods

November 2—Buckingham executed at Salisbury

1484
Edward, Prince of Wales, son of Richard III, dies

1485
Henry Tudor lands with army on Welsh coast (August 7); Richard III killed at Battle of Bosworth (August 22); Tudor is crowned as King Henry VII

1674
Skeletons thought to be those of the princes are found under staircase in Tower of London (July 17)

For Further Reading

Clifford Lindsey Alderman, *Blood Red the Roses*. New York: Julian Messner, 1971. Highly readable account of the Wars of the Roses. Short on pictures, but includes bibliography, index, and suggestions for further reading.

Janice Young Brooks, *Kings and Queens: The Plantagenets of England*. Nashville, TN: Thomas Nelson, 1975. This lively telling of the lives and times of the Plantagenets was originally published in 1883. Roughly half the book deals with the rulers during the Wars of the Roses.

Robert Louis Stevenson, *Black Arrow*. New York: St. Martin's Press, 1965. Action-packed novel about the exploits of a young knight set loosely against the background of the Wars of the Roses.

Marguerite Vance, *Song for a Lute*. New York: E. P. Dutton, 1958. Highly fictionalized biography of Anne Neville. Almost ignores deaths of Edward IV's sons.

Jan Westcott, *Set Her on a Throne*. Boston: Little, Brown, 1972. Fictional story of the life of Anne Neville, the earl of Warwick's daughter and Richard III's queen, from 1470 until her death. Highly accurate in historical details.

Sylvia Wright, *The Age of Chivalry: English Society 1200–1400*. New York: Warwick Press, 1988. Well-illustrated social and political history of England in the Middle Ages. Provides good background for the Wars of the Roses.

Works Consulted

Oscar James Campbell, ed., *The Living Shakespeare*. New York: Macmillan, 1958. A collection of twenty-two plays and the sonnets of Shakespeare, each accompanied by an essay detailing its history.

Thomas B. Costain, *The Last Plantagenets*. Garden City, NY: Doubleday, 1962. Last of four volumes in the author's Pageant of England series. Reads like a novel, with liberal doses of the author's opinion, but soundly grounded in fact.

James Gairdner, *History of the Life and Reign of Richard the Third*. New York: Greenwood Press, 1969. This reprinting of a biography first published in 1898 blames Richard for the princes' deaths.

Franklin Hamilton, *Challenge for a Throne: The Wars of the Roses.* New York: Dial Press, 1967. Fast-moving, highly entertaining account of the period, but lack of footnotes is a handicap to the serious student.

Michael Hicks, *Richard III: The Man Behind the Myth.* London: Collins and Brown, 1991. Attempts to ignore some of the more biased negative stories of Richard's life and reign to give a factual account concentrating on his accomplishments.

George Holmes, *The Later Middle Ages: 1272–1485.* New York: W. W. Norton, 1962. Third volume in the Norton History of England series. Good summary of politics and events in England.

David Hume, *The History of England from the Invasion of Julius Caesar to the Revolution of 1688.* Boston: Little, Brown, 1854. This massive, six-volume classic of English history is now somewhat antiquated, but remains a good source for dates and facts.

Elizabeth Jenkins, *The Princes in the Tower.* New York: Coward McCann & Coohagen, 1978. A thorough examination of all the evidence, particularly of the bones found in the Tower of London, that concludes that Richard III probably murdered the princes.

Paul Murray Kendall, *Richard the Third.* New York: W. W. Norton, 1956. This biography, while not ignoring the darker side of Richard's character, takes pains to show his positive traits.

Paul Murray Kendall, ed., *The Great Debate.* New York: W. W. Norton, 1965. Kendall presents both sides of the debate over the guilt of Richard III in this combination of Sir Thomas More's *History of King Richard III* and Horace Walpole's *Historic Doubts.*

J. R. Lander, *The Wars of the Roses.* New York: G. P. Putnam's Sons, 1966. The story of the wars and the surrounding political events is told through the words of writers of the time—in letters, diary entries, chronicles, and legal proceedings. Lengthy passages in antiquated language can be tedious.

Dominic Mancini, *The Usurpation of Richard the Third.* Translated by C. A. J. Armstrong. Oxford: Clarendon Press, 1969. English translation of Mancini's report written in 1483 but not discovered until 1936. Important because it gives the unbiased observations of a foreigner.

A. R. Myers, ed., *English Historical Documents: 1327–1485.* New York: Oxford University Press, 1969. The fourth in a multivolume series offering translations of all or part of documents written during the period. Includes everything from treaties to the cost of breakfast for the king's council.

Charles Ross, *Richard III.* Berkeley: University of California Press,

1981. Highly accurate and detailed biography of Richard, although it often assumes that readers have a considerable familiarity with the story.

A. L. Rowse, *Bosworth Field: From Medieval to Tudor England.* Garden City, NY: Doubleday, 1966. Part of the Crossroads of World History series. Despite the title, this is a full account of events from the overthrow of Richard II in 1399 to the early years of the reign of Henry VII.

———, *The Tower of London in the History of England.* New York: G. P. Putnam's Sons, 1982. Meticulously documented and well-illustrated history of the Tower from its building under William the Conqueror to present times.

Desmond Seward, *Richard III: England's Black Legend.* New York: Franklin Watts, 1984. This exceptionally well written and lively story of Richard's reign lays the princes' deaths squarely on their uncle.

Giles St. Aubyn, *The Year of Three Kings.* New York: Atheneum, 1983. Good, comprehensive account of the year 1483, in which three kings—Edward IV, Edward V, and Richard III—lived.

George M. Trevelyan, *A Shortened History of England.* Harmondsworth, England: Penguin Books, 1962. Has been called the best single-volume history of England ever written, and with good reason. Marvelous writer gives all the whos, whens, and wheres along with the hows and whys.

Polydore Vergil, *Three Books of Polydore Vergil's English History.* Edited by Sir Henry Ellis. London: John Bowyer Nichols and Son, 1844. The period of Vergil's history covering the reigns of Henry VI, Edward IV, and Richard III from a very early English translation from the Latin.

Alison Weir, *The Princes in the Tower.* New York: Ballantine Books, 1992. This excellent account of the events surrounding the deaths of Edward IV's young sons in the Tower of London lays the blame directly at the feet of Richard III.

Audrey Williamson, *The Mystery of the Princes.* Chicago: Academy Chicago Publishers, 1992. A thorough examination of the disappearance and presumed murders of the young Edward V and his brother the duke of York. The author seeks to cast doubt on the traditional belief that the princes were murdered by their uncle Richard III.

Derek Wilson, *The Tower.* New York: Charles Scribner's Sons, 1979. A thorough history of the Tower of London but not nearly as well illustrated as Rowse's book.

Index

Picture Credits

About the Author

William W. Lace is a native of Fort Worth, Texas. He holds a bache-
lor's degree from Texas Christian University, a master's degree from
East Texas State University, and a doctorate from the University of
North Texas. After writing for newspapers in Baytown, Texas, and
Fort Worth, he joined the University of Texas at Arlington, eventually becoming director of the News Service. He is now vice chancellor for public affairs ar Tarrant County Junior College in Fort
Worth. His love of English history began at age five when he discovered his father's old book of King Arthur stories in an attic. He
has written eleven books for Lucent, most dealing with England
and Great Britain. He and his wife Laura, a school librarian, live in
Arlington, Texas, and have two grown children.